To
Joan

The Price of Wisdom

Best wishes

Kate Townsend

The Price of Wisdom

Kate Townsend

ATHENA PRESS
LONDON

THE PRICE OF WISDOM
Copyright © Kate Townsend 2009

ISBN 978 1 84748 610 3

First published 2009 by
ATHENA PRESS
Queen's House, 2 Holly Road
Twickenham TW1 4EG
United Kingdom

Every effort has been made to trace the copyright holders
of works quoted within this book and obtain permission. The
publisher apologises for any omission and is happy to make
necessary changes in subsequent print runs.

Printed for Athena Press

Introduction

Kate's mission in life was to heal her broken heart. She prayed for the wisdom to help her make sense of it all.

Little did she know that to acquire wisdom, you need first to experience being unwise. Just as you cannot know the meaning of light until you experienced the dark.

Everything has its opposite, like love and hate. How can one choose what one wants in life until one knows what one doesn't want? The two have to be together for one to be able to decide.

Here is a proverb I like to tell:

The young boy said to the old wise man, 'Please tell me, old man, how do you acquire wisdom?'

'Come with me to the riverbank and I will show you,' said the old man.

The boy followed the old wise man to the riverbank and when he got there, the old wise man said, 'Kneel down and look into the river.'

The boy did what he said and knelt down to look into the river.

The old wise man put his hand on his head and pushed the boy's head under the water. He held it down in the water for a few moments and then let him go. The boy gasped for air and said, 'Why did you do that?'

The old wise man said, 'When you are gasping for wisdom, as you are now gasping for air, that is when you will acquire it.'

All the hardships and tribulations Kate endured became the source of wisdom and strength that arose from her experiences.

It was as if a trapdoor opened when Kate reached the rock bottom in life.

Her life then slowly changed for the better when she found the twelve-step recovery programme.

This book is about Kate's recovery; recovery from the pain from co-dependency, low self-esteem and shame.

~1~

It was the beginning of the war when I was born. Not a good time, as everyone was worried about what was going to happen with Germany. It was a very uneasy time in the world. Britain was facing the danger of invasion and occupation.

I was evacuated to the country with my mother, my sister Rosy and brother Billy, for the first three years of my life. I stayed in a cottage, 'Rose Cottage', in a little rural village named Bottesford, in Leicestershire.

The country life for us kids was a good thing. We loved the open countryside, where we were free to grow and play safely. Did I say safely?

I was trailing behind my family as we were walking across the fields of the farmland one day, when suddenly my mother shouted, 'Run, Kate, run!'

I looked over my shoulder and there was this great big animal with its head low and angry eyes that were gazing at me. I heard my mother's voice again. 'Run, Kate!'

My mother and siblings were on the other side of a fence beckoning me to run towards them. I was petrified and started to run with all the strength that a three-year-old could muster up. I darted under that fence like a bullet. The bull was close behind me.

'It must have been your red skirt, Kate, that he was after!' my mother said with a chuckle. I couldn't see the funny side of it.

This was one of my earliest memories as a child: being chased by a bull, would you believe it!

It was January 1944 when my mother decided to come home. She was fed up with the quiet life and missed her family in London.

We were a close family. There was my grandmother, Jane, known as Janey (she was 'Nanny' to me). Then came Freddie, Mum's brother; Lou was the eldest sister. My mother, Hettie, was next in line; she was called 'Et' for short. Beth came next, then May; she was the youngest. I never got to meet my grandfathers.

We stayed with Aunt Lou, until my mother found a place of our own to live.

I was coming up to four years old and could remember clearly the day when my mother found the house that we lived in for many years that followed.

The weather was very cold, and it had been snowing. My mother walked the streets for days. Her feet were freezing. The snow got through her worn shoes and her toes were numb with the cold. Stamping her feet to keep the circulation working, and blowing into her cold hands, she saw the 'To Let' sign.

At last, she found a two-bed flat, upstairs in a terraced house not far from where my nanny lived.

'I've got some rooms, Mum.'

'Oh, that's good, Et. Whereabouts?' Nanny said.

'Thorpedale Road.'

'Where's that?'

'It's about fifteen minutes' walk away.'

My mother was relieved to have her own home at last. It was a bit tight at Aunt Lou's house; she had two boys of her own to cope with.

'How yer gonna get yer furniture over there, Et?' Freddie said.

'Dunno, Fred. Wanna give us a hand?'

'How much yer got?'

'Coupla beds, armchair, wardrobe – yer know, bits and pieces.'

'Well, all right then, I'll ask me mate if I can borrow his wheelbarrow. When d'yer wanna move?'

'As soon as yer can, Fred. Tomorrow, if it ain't snowing.'

Freddie turned up at Aunt Lou's house at ten o'clock the next morning. He brought Harry with him. He was married to Aunt Beth – Uncle Harry, so to speak.

The day was bright and cold. It wasn't snowing, thank God, but there was a bit of snow on the ground. Fortunately, it wasn't freezing, just slushy and wet.

Rosy helped out by loading up my old pram. She was coming up to twelve and Billy, my brother, was nine.

'C'mon, Et, push it! It'll keep yer fit,' Freddie said jokingly.

'Yer look like the old iron man, Fred.'

'Yeah, any old iron. He called out, 'Any old iron!' raising his voice.

'Hush, you're showing me up!' my mother said, giving him a friendly clip round his ear with her headscarf. The ladies wore scarves around their heads in those days, or they made a turban out of it with a couple of curlers sticking out the front. I can remember my mother with her scarf tied and up wearing an apron over her forties-style dress.

Fred was fun-loving, just like his father was, and being an ex-newspaper boy, he knew how to call out and be heard.

'Got plenty of old iron 'ere, cheap as chips!'

'Hush, Freddie! Don't mess about,' my mother said, but couldn't help laughing and expressing her feelings. 'Yer remind me of yer dad, Fred!'

He gave her an affectionate smile and said, 'Well, let's get yer sorted, cock, so we can get the kids settled.'

For the last haul, I was in the old pram with a blanket wrapped around me with our gas masks piled on top.

'Mum, I'm freezing,' Rosy said.

'So am I,' Billy complained.

'Won't be long now. I'll light a nice fire when we get settled.'

Aunt Lou lived in Archway, which was about two miles away. It took all day, back and forth, to move our furniture from her house to ours.

'Blimey, Et, that was hard work! 'Ave yer got any milk? I fancy a nice cuppa Rosie Lee.'

'Thanks, Fred, and you too, Harry. I don't know what I would 'ave done wivout yer,' my mother said as she put the kettle on the old gas stove.

At last, we settled down in our new home. Everyone was exhausted.

My mother was missing my father, who was still overseas serving in the army. It was amazing how hardly anyone during the war gave in to the hardships that wartime brought.

The spirit of the community brought out the best in us all. The good humour manifested itself in such sayings as, 'Don't you know there's a war on?' People just got on with it. All the dangers and the many shortages, the rationing and the dreadful blackouts, all became a way of life. Strangely enough, it brought the community closer together. We were like one big family out to help one another on a daily basis.

It took some weeks to settle down. I hated London. The houses were so close together and the school building was old and big. When I looked up, the moving clouds in the sky gave me the feeling that the school building was going to fall down on top of me.

'Turn the wireless on, Mum; I fink *Children's Hour*'s on now,' Billy said.

The programmes, *Just William* and Arthur Askey were our favourites. I was too young at that time to know what it was all about. You could say I was a bit of a pain in the arse to my siblings.

The wireless was a lifesaver. The BBC had a station with programmes that became very important for the morale of the people, such as *Children's Hour, Women's Hour, Forces Favourites* and *Music while you Work*. But the most popular programme of all was *ITMA* ('It's That Man Again') starring Tommy Hanley. It was full of humour and sketches, making fun of everyone involved in the war. It was so good for the spirit of the nation. The wireless was a great comfort to my mother and us kids.

Sometimes my mother told stories about her childhood days. Rosy and Billy often encouraged her to tell us a story. It was one of my dearest memories as a child. I was very young, but could remember her stories for ever.

Her mind was always running away with her. Some of her stories were true; some she made up. The way she told them was magical, and her lovely green eyes shone. She enchanted the listeners into the world of her imagination.

I'd sit by the fireside, watching the flickering flames, and be fascinated with the colours and shapes of the fire burning, wondering what life was all about. I wasn't aware of what path my life was going to take then, being only four years old. I was a bit confused. One minute I was in the country where there was open space and green fields. We lived near a farm that had cows and sheep in the fields – not forgetting the bulls. There was a dog and a cat that I played with. Then suddenly here I was back in a small room with nowhere to play.

'Want some toast, Kate?'

'Mmm, please, Mum.'

She got out the long fork from the kitchen draw, stuck the bread on the end, and then held it in front of the open fire, being careful not to burn her hand. Sometimes the bread fell off the fork. But that didn't matter; she'd dust the ash off, then spread on the rationed butter and offer it to me.

' 'Ere y'are, Kate. Be careful, it's hot.'

'Thanks, Mum.'

We tucked in to the ashy tasting toast, waiting for our mother to start her story. Rosy and Billy sat with anticipation, tucking into their toast and drinking cocoa made from water.

No matter how many times my mother told the same old stories, we never got tired of listening.

'Now, are you comfortable?

'Mmm,' I said, wiping my hands and mouth with the teacloth.

'Good, then I will begin,' said my mum.

'Once upon a time there was a man named Alfie…'

~2~

Alfie Jones was the eldest son of George and Emily Jones. George was a miner in Wales. His mother, Emily, was born in London.

They married and raised their family in Wales. But Emily didn't want her sons to follow in their father's footsteps, because she hated being a miner's wife, so they all moved back to London and lived in Highgate.

Alfie had two brothers, Billy and Jimmy, and two sisters, Megan and Charlotte.

George rented a yard in Holloway Road. He bought a horse and cart and began selling coal from door to door with his sons.

They were known as the Coalman Brothers.

Alfie was the eldest. He was nearly seventeen, a tough lad, with built-up muscles due to lifting heavy coal sacks. His eyes were as black as the coal he delivered. His hair was dark and a little curly; a very handsome boy. He was full of energy and always up to mischief. His younger brothers looked up to him as their hero.

One of his favourite stunts was sticking a coin on the ground and waiting for someone to try to pick it up; he'd be cracking himself with laughter. He had so much charisma; he could charm the boots off you.

Alfie didn't have a care it the world until he met Jane.

Jane came from a well-to-do family. Her mother had died when she was born. Her stepmother suppressed her as she was growing up; this was due to her being jealous of the relationship she had with her father. Her stepbrother and stepsister were sly and crafty; they made her feel inferior to them.

Jane lived in a town house, in Hampstead. The servants' quarters were downstairs. Some of the maids lived in the attic.

The only person Jane really cared for was her nanny, Dorothy, whom she adored. She called her 'Doodee'.

Dorothy was Jane's nanny since she was born. She came from

Ireland. She was a small lady, with a strong mind and a loving heart.

'Jane, now will yer stand still, child! How d'ye t'ink I can get yer hem straight if ye don't keep still?' Doodee said with pins in her mouth, trying to shorten Jane's dress.

'Sorry, Doodee, I was trying to see out of the window. There are some women down there, Doodee. They look like the suffragette women.'

Emmeline Pankhurst was one of the founders of the movement that had been campaigning since 1889 for women's voting rights.

'Oh, Mary, mother of God! Just look at the kerfuffle going on down dere! Bejasus, you'd t'ink dere was a war on!'

Jane was attracted by the propaganda of the suffragette movement, but Emmeline Pankhurst's tactics for drawing attention to her women's rights movement led her to being imprisoned.

She went on hunger strike many times and was force-fed. Jane thought she was a brave lady and held the greatest admiration for her.

Henry Wilson, Jane's father, was very adamant about her not getting involved with the campaign.

He was a hard man; all he thought about was making money. He owned a spinning and weaving mill in the Midlands.

When the sewing machine was invented, he moved to Hampstead and opened a factory in Hornsey Road making children's clothes.

He exploited the poor for cheap labour. But thanks to the rise of the British Trade Union movement, the strikes, the hardships and self-sacrificing that went on to settle their differences came under control. The new laws were made and the employees were given a voice to be heard and could bargain with their employers.

Jane was coming up to seventeen. She was a rebellious child, and didn't agree with her father's principles.

On Sunday afternoon, Jane went for a ride with Doodee to Hyde Park.

'Come on, Doodee, let's stop here and go for a walk,' Jane said.

'Well, all right, Jane dear, but don't you be getting involved with the ladies in groups now. Your father made it clear that you must keep away.'

'Don't worry, Doodee – I just want to go for a little stroll.'

The carriage pulled up and the coachman helped Jane and Doodee alight. Jane was dressed in green that day with a bonnet to match, which made the colour of her green eyes stand out even more.

Off they strolled along the pathway leading to the corner where people spoke their points of view on all kinds of subjects.

Alfie first saw Jane when he was delivering coal to their house. He was offered a cup of tea and was invited in to join the servants in the kitchen.

The staff loved him because he'd brighten up their day with his charm.

Sometimes, Jane came down into the kitchen to see Mrs Todd, the cook.

Alfie was sipping his tea when Jane came in. He fell in love with her the moment he first set eyes on her.

Mrs Todd knew how unhappy Jane was, because she'd made a friend of Doodee. She told her how her stepmother treated her.

Mrs Todd felt sorry for Jane and made a fuss of her. She cooked her special little treats to cheer her up.

Jane loved to slip away to the kitchen to be with servants. She was more at home with the staff than when mixing with the gentry. She was as happy as a pea in a pod when she was in the kitchen.

Alfie had his eye on her for a long time, and when he heard how unhappy she was, he thought, She's the one for me.

He'd spruce himself up and wait on the corner of her road, hoping she'd come out of the house. But she was always chaperoned by her nanny.

'Yer've gotta be off yer trolley, Alf! She'd not be innerested in yer, she's to posh for yer. 'Er old man won't let yer near 'er,' said Billy, Alfie's brother.

'Don't care! I've set me sights on 'er and... just you wait and see,' Alfie said with a look of determination on his face.

At first, Jane wasn't interested in Alfie. She was always to busy talking about the women's rights campaign with Mrs Todd.

He soon learned that they went to Hyde Park on a Sunday afternoon. Alfie, being a smart lad, went to the park and waited for her horse and carriage to arrive.

There it was, just pulling up on the side of the path. He watched them alight from the carriage, and thought, 'Ere's me chance to talk to 'er. He hid behind the big oak tree and waited for Jane to pass.

'I'll just take a rest here, Jane. Don't you go very far, now,' Doodee said as she sat down on the park bench.

'Don't worry, Doodee, I won't.'

Doodee had a little doze and Alfie saw his opportunity.

'Good afternoon, Miss Wilson.' He bowed a little, holding his hat in his hand. His smile was enchanting, with teeth so even and white; as he smiled the sunlight caught the glint in his eyes. Jane recognised him and said, 'Good afternoon to you, Alfie.'

Every Sunday afternoon, Alfie went to Hyde Park in the hope of seeing Jane.

He did all sorts of things to attract her attention. Once he made out he'd tripped over a stone. The next week he was flying a kite. He even tried making out he was a busker by juggling coloured balls and dropping them everywhere.

One time he hired a penny-farthing bike for the afternoon. That was quite a challenge. He fell off, right in front of Jane.

It took him six weeks to get her to look forward to seeing him again in the park.

Every Sunday afternoon, around three thirty, Alfie waited for her. He got out his fob watch to see what the time was. 'Hmm, three thirty, she should be 'ere by now,' he whispered to himself.

There she was, walking along with her chaperone, Doodee. She looked a picture, strolling along dressed in a blue satin dress with a sailor's collar trimmed with lace. She had a hat to match her dress, dainty lace gloves and white shoes with little buttons on the side. She was holding a white lace parasol, her head on a little tilt, trying not to let Doodee see that she was looking for Alfie.

Her heart skipped when she saw him leaning against the big oak tree. He was smiling like a Cheshire cat, with his arms folded and one leg crossed over the other.

They waited until Doodee dozed off on the park bench, then they'd sneak away around the big oak tree, messing around and chasing each other. They were as innocent as children playing. They would make daisy chains, and spend the time hiding and talking about their dreams.

One day, Alfie climbed the tree when Jane wasn't looking and surprised her by jumping behind her, making her jump.

Jane fell for his charms and strong personality.

'Oh, Alfie, you do make me laugh! I can't remember ever having so much fun,' Jane said.

Alfie stood looking into her green bewitching eyes and slowly lent closer. He paused for a moment, not sure if she would be angry if he kissed her. His heart started to beat faster; he was totally powerless to control his desire to kiss her, and then he gently kissed her on her lips. She didn't pull away; he pulled her close and held her in his arms. They kissed passionately.

At that moment in time, Alfie felt all the emotions that he had suppressed since he first saw her, and his heart felt as if it was going to explode.

Jane flushed and took a pace back. She knew that she was falling in love for the first in her life.

'Oh, Alfie, I do love you!' she said, and kissed him back.

'I love you too, Janey!' They kissed again. Alfie's eyes looked deep into Jane's. They were experiencing the power of nature drawing them together.

Jane became afraid of her feelings. It was the first time that she felt the sexual energies charging through her body.

'I must get back to Doodee – she'll be worried about me. See you next Sunday!' She was gone in a flash.

Alfie shouted out loud, 'She loves me!' He danced all the way home. He was hopelessly in love.

Six months later, still secretly meeting in Hyde Park, Alfie said to Jane, 'Janey, I'm gonna ask yer father if I can marry yer.'

'Oh, no, Alfie, he'll throw you out!' Jane said, with fear in her eyes.

'I ain't afraid of no man! He can only say no, and that will be that. At least I asked him,' Alfie replied, and made an appointment to see her father the next day.

'Mr Alfred Jones to see you, sir,' said the butler, holding the door open for Alfie to enter.

Mr Wilson was standing with his back against the open fire, holding his fob watch. He was a stout man with a rather large moustache. He put his fob pocket watch back into his pocket and said, 'Come in, boy, and close the door. You're the young coalman, aren't you?' He lifted his monocle, recognising him. 'What do you want?'

Alfie cleared his throat and gave a little cough.

'Good evening, Mr Wilson,' he said timidly, holding his hat in his hand. 'I've –' he held up his chin – 'I've come to ask, sir...'

Mr Wilson looked stern and was frowning. 'Speak up, lad; you've come to ask what?'

Alfie was feeling a little embarrassed. 'If you wouldn't mind, sir, I would like to marry Jane.' He'd said it.

Mr Wilson went berserk.

'Certainly not, boy! I will not allow my daughter to marry beneath her. I forbid you to see her again. If you do, I will cut off her allowance and disown her. Do you hear me? Now get out!'

Alfie went, leaving Mr Wilson grumbling to himself, 'What's the boy thinking of?' He shook his head from side to side.

'Jane!' he shouted. 'Send Jane to me, Hudson,' he said to the butler.

When Jane came in, he said, 'How long has this been going on? What do you think you're doing, girl? He's a coalman!'

'I'm sorry, Father,' Jane said with a tremble in her voice. She was afraid of her father. 'I love him and want to be with him.'

'Over my dead body! You're a fool. Don't you know how embarrassing this is for me? If it got out that my daughter was engaged to a coalman, I would be a laughing stock. I forbid you to see him again. Now go to your room and stay there until I say otherwise.'

Jane hung her head down and went to her room with her eyes full of tears.

She fell into Doodee's arms and cried.

'There, there, child. Don't you be getting yourself upset. Now, tell me what's the matter.'

Jane blurted out through her sobs, 'I can't help loving him, Doodee.' Then she told her what had been going on the last six months.

'I know, dear, I wasn't always sleeping,' said her kind nanny. She went on, 'Listen, Jane dear, I know how unhappy ye are here, wit' yer stepmother and her spoilt brats. If ye do decide to leave and marry dat boy, I have me savings ye can have. It 'ud help ye start yer own life.'

Dorothy went to her secret hiding place and brought out an old tin. She handed Jane her life savings, which was quite a substantial amount: £100.

Jane gave Doodee a hug and said, 'Oh, Doodee, thank you! Thank you! But what will happen to you?'

'Don't ye be worrin' yer pretty little head about me. I will go to me sister's in Devon. I'm getting old now and ready to retire. You're everyt'ing to me, child, I've loved ye as if ye were me own daughter. Now, my sweet girl, what are ye goin' to do?'

Alfie didn't expect any different from Mr Wilson, but he had to ask, to satisfy himself that he had tried.

He proposed to Jane anyway.

'Janey – it's me or yer family. I can't give yer a house like ye're used to, but I will look after yer. I do love yer, I love yer wiv all me heart. I'd be lost wivout yer. Will yer marry me?' Alfie was on one knee with a small diamond ring in his hand that he had being saving up for, hoping Jane would accept his proposal of marriage.

Jane was overjoyed when Alfie proposed, but she was also very nervous, knowing what the consequences were if she accepted.

Jane made her decision to run away and marry Alfie. She was so much in love with him. He was so much fun and he made her laugh.

Her life with her father and stepfamily was sad; the only one she cared about was Doodee.

Jane left carrying only the old tin box Doodee gave her with £100 inside. She had a picture of her mother and one of herself and Doodee, a cape and a few clothes.

'Goodbye, Doodee. Please come to visit me.'

'Goodbye, my little sweet child. Be happy… of course I will, as soon as I get settled.' Doodee wiped her eyes and prayed, 'Take care of my baby, God.'

Alfie and Jane were married in 1906.

Her father stuck to his word and cut her off from her inheritance. She never saw him again.

Jane put the money that Doodee gave her in a bank account and bought a terrace house in Finsbury Park. It was just around the corner from Alfie's family.

She bought fine furniture and a piano. She could play the piano quite well. Jane went from a cold, unloving house into a loving home.

The Jones family adored her.

She taught Alfie's sisters to embroider and make clothes, and brought music into their lives with her piano playing.

In return, they showed Jane how to laugh and be a part of a loving family.

~3~

'Did they live happily ever after?' I said.

My mother gave me a smile as if to say, I'm glad you enjoyed my story, and then said, 'Yes, but there's more, I'll tell you all about it next time. It's getting late now and I must get your dinner ready.'

Suddenly, she stood up. Her face went white and then she said, 'Quick! It's the warning siren, there's going to be a raid.'

'Mum, run to the shelter!' Rosy cried fearfully.

Then there was the sound of engines flying over head. The look on my mother's face put the fear of God into me.

'Under the table! It's too late to get to the shelter.'

We all scrambled under the table. Then there was an almighty explosion, and the house shock.

'That was close!' Mum said.

I gazed into my mother's face, looking for the relief from the fear she was feeling. Then came another explosion. This time it was farther away.

After ten minutes of kneeling on all fours, we came out from under the table and felt a cold chill. All the windows were blown out. A bomb had hit our road.

'Thank God we didn't go to the shelter! We would have all been caught in the blast. Come on, kids, we're going to Grandma's. We can't stay here. Put your coat on, Rose. Billy, get the pram out.'

Then she remembered the gas masks and called, 'Get your gas mask too.'

We were running about gathering our things like headless chickens.

I was shivering with the cold and shock. The fear went through my body like wildfire. This was the first time I'd experienced a raid.

The all-clear siren was still wailing as we all gathered around my pram, making our way through the debris to my nanny's house.

Beth and Harry lived with my grandmother. Their two children, Jimmy and Jessie, were still evacuees in the country.

I was feeling a lot better now. The fear had gone from Mother's face.

I was in my pram on my way to my nanny's, when I looked up and saw searchlights crossing each other in the black night sky. The air was full of smoke, with the smell of burning. This raid wiped out three houses in our road. Billy and Rosy held on to the pram as we went past what was left of them. They had taken a direct hit.

'Oh, dear!' my mother said. 'Just look at that, one of those houses is Teddy's house, Kate's little playmate.'

My mother was trembling all over, and it wasn't from the cold. She was suffering from shock.

The scene that night brought home the reality of the war and how quickly it takes life. I heard my mother say, 'This could have been me.' The tears rolled down her face thinking of little Teddy. He was playing with me only yesterday morning.

As we approached the road my nanny lived in, Mum was relieved to see Beth, Harry and Nanny.

'Beth!' she called out. They were walking back from the underground station.

'Hello, Et! That was a bad raid – you all right?'

'Mmm… got no windows, though.'

'Oh, dear. Come on in, I'll put the kettle on. Have yer eaten?' Beth said as she was opening the front door.

'No, not yet.'

'Don't worry. Harry!' she called out. 'See if the fish and chip shop is open and get us something to eat.'

'Make yerself at home, Et,' Beth added.

'You all right, Mum?' my mother asked Nanny.

'Yes, I'm all right, Et. You should have stayed in the country, you were much safer there.'

'I know, Mum, but it was so lonely.'

'I know, duck, we missed you too.'

The raid didn't stop life from carrying on, no matter what the damage. It didn't break people's spirit, whatever the dangers; therefore, the fish and chip shop was open.

Harry got out the ration coupons and went off to get our supper.

A little later on Harry came rushing in the door, shouting, 'Quick! We must leave – there's an unexploded mine bomb at the top of our road. The whole road has to evacuate.'

'Oh, bloody hell!' my mother sighed. She grabbed us kids and called up to Nanny, who lived upstairs, 'C'mon, Mum, we have to go! There's a bomb in our road that could go off at any moment!'

'Oh, dear, I'll get my coat.'

'Don't forget your gas mask!' Beth called.

Once again, Mum put me in the pram, gathered Rosy and Billy, and we all set off for the underground station carrying our gas masks and the chips.

The station was crowded; people were spread out everywhere. We made ourselves comfortable on the platform and waited.

'Have you heard from May?' my mother asked Beth.

'Yeah, she's on leave this weekend. She wrote that she's got something important to tell us.'

I remembered my Aunt May very well; she was the one who showed me a lot of love and affection when I was a baby.

She often came to visit us when we were evacuated. I loved her very much and was excited to hear that she was coming to see us soon. She was in the NAAFI working in the canteens.

'She'll be real happy to see you, Et,' Beth said, passing her a chip.

May and my mother were like best friends as well as sisters; they were very close. My mother hadn't seen her since we came home from the country.

'Did yer hear about our Freddie, Et?' Beth said.

'No. Why, is he all right?'

'Oh, yeah, he's fine. He met someone…'

'No! Who?'

'An American journalist, her name's Susan.'

'Where did he meet her?'

'Well, yer know how he's working with the newspapers. She

was in London writing a story about the war and that. Well, she was interviewing Freddie. Then there was a raid. They both went down into the shelter for a while. She got a bit scared, as she'd never experienced a raid before. She held on to Freddie, and he took a fancy to her,' Beth went on to say. 'He's going to America with her.'

'Is that right, Beth? Well, well, I hope he finds happiness with her. He's been on his own now for far too long.'

'Yeah, so do I,' Beth said.

'What does Lou think about it?'

'You know what's she like, don't trust no one. She says yer must look before yer leap, and don't rush into anything.'

'Well, he hasn't known her for long. To go to America is a big decision to make. I guess she's only looking out for him. I think he's big enough to know what he's doing. Besides, yer have to grab happiness while yer can, yer don't know what tomorrow brings.'

Beth agreed, and looked over to her mother. 'You OK, Mum?'

' 'Course I am! Don't you be worrying about me, just look after the young 'uns. God bless them, it must be horrible for them with all this commotion going on in their young lives. It reminds me of the days when your father was in the war and I was left to take care of you all by myself. All I hope is, we have a home to go back to.'

Nanny was getting on a bit now, but she still had her inner spirit. She was a great lady. 'You have to be strong,' she always said.

'I think we might have to stay down here for the night. There's a hammock over there; I'll grab it for Katie.' My mother sorted me out and we all settled down and slept the night on the platform.

Time passed by slowly. We couldn't sleep very well, what with all the coughing and snoring from so many people sleeping together.

Some of them were singing old-time music hall songs. I heard my mother say, 'You have to be strong, and singing helps to keep up our morale.'

'Yes, so it does, Et,' Nanny said, and then joined in with the others.

'There'll be bluebirds over the white cliffs of Dover, some day, just you wait and see...'

I fell asleep in my little hammock, content and feeling safe. It had been a long day.

At six in the morning, Mum said, 'C'mon, Beth, I'm off. Can't stay down here any longer. Rosy, you awake?'

Rosy sat up rubbing her eyes and said, 'Mum, I need to go,' crossing her legs with a worried look on her face.

'Billy, wake up, love! Won't be long, Rosy, we're going now.'

She got me from the hammock and, stepping over the sleeping people, made her way to the exit. Beth, Harry and Nanny following behind. We all made straight for the toilets.

The mine bomb had been defused and everyone went on with their daily routine.

My mother got her windows replaced by the landlord and we all moved back home.

Aunt May came home on leave and told my mother that she was pregnant.

'What! Oh, May, what will Jack say?'

'I don't know, Et!'

'How far gone are yer?'

'A couple of months, I suppose.'

'Come 'ere, May!' My mother gave her sister a cuddle.

I was told years later that my Aunt May had four miscarriages and a baby girl who only lived for three months. All she ever wanted was a baby, and now she was pregnant by some Yank who she'd probably never see again.

'What shall I do, Et? I don't want to get rid of it, I might be lucky this time.'

'Keep it, May. If you like, I'll write and let Jack know.' (Jack was May's husband; he was in the army overseas somewhere.)

'No, not yet,' May sighed.

'Why don't you stay with us until you get yourself sorted?'

'Thanks, Et, I think I will.'

'Come on, Kate, it's getting late,' my mother said, then she went outside to find Rosy and Billy, they were playing in the street.

'Rosy, Billy!' Mum called.

'Can we stay out a little longer? We're playing "kerb and the old brick wall".' That was one of the street games the kids played.

'OK, but be in by eight the latest, if yer want to go to the Saturday morning flicks, or yer'll be too tired to get up.'

'Mum, will yer tell me a story before I go to bed? I want to know what happened to Alfie and Jane,' I said.

'Well, OK, get washed and put yer nightie on. I'll make yer some cocoa.'

We made ourselves comfortable by the fireside. I sat opposite Mum on a small armchair.

'Are you comfortable?'

'Mmm,' I said, feeling cosy.

'Well, then, I will begin.'

~4~

A year after Alfie and Jane were married, along came the first of the babies. Freddie was born first, then Louise, then Hettie.

All the family pulled together to help out with the children. Sometimes Doodee came up from Devon to help out. She lived by the sea with her two sisters.

Alfie worked with his father and brothers. The coal business was just making a living.

Jane gave piano lessons to earn a little extra cash. She was happy and content because she always had her family around her.

The old cliché, 'You can't beat the Joneses' certainly applied with this family at that time.

On the 4 August 1914, Britain declared war on Germany.

No one took it seriously and everyone was so excited about going to war. Crowds gathered outside Buckingham Palace, cheering and singing the National Anthem.

Everyone thought it was going to be a great adventure. All the young men were anxious not to miss the war, which was thought would be over by Christmas.

They all queued to sign up. Young men came from all over Britain to join up. Even boys who were at school gave false ages in order to enlist.

They thought nothing of the hardships and dangers that they would face. They all thought this war was going to be an excuse for a break from their boring everyday existence.

Alfie and his brothers were among the men in the queue, just as eager as the rest.

Jane was broken-hearted to think that Alfie would join up and leave her, especially since she was pregnant again. But she couldn't show how she felt because all the women were encouraged to support the men. Alfie really thought that he would be back before Christmas.

'Alfie, take care of yourself and promise me you will come home.'

'Don't worry, Janey, I'll be back in a few weeks.'

Alfie held her in his arms, kissed her and went off with his brothers, totally unaware of what lay before them.

Two years passed before Jane saw Alfie again.

Jane's life turned around the day Alfie left. All the fun when out of her existence. She had another girl. They named her Elizabeth; Beth for short.

George and Emily were a great support to Jane and her children, but she missed Alfie so much. She missed his sense of humour and support.

The war went on and on. The hardships the men endured were unbelievable. Many young men never came back.

Europe counted the cost of the war: 10 million dead. It was almost a lost generation.

Gray, the Foreign Secretary at the time, said when the war was declared, 'The lamps are going out over all Europe; we shall not see them lit again in our lifetime.' He wasn't wrong. The war at last came to an end in November 1918.

Alfie came home in 1916 because he was badly wounded. The scars healed in time, but the mental scars were a different story.

He wasn't the same man who had kissed Jane goodbye that day back in 1914. He had suffered far more than he could ever have imagined.

The days and nights stuck in muddy trenches, the starvation and the cold – he was very near to death himself. He lost his free-spirited nature, and when he heard the news about his brothers his heart broke.

They were both killed serving their king and country.

Alfie started to drink and spent most of the time in the pub.

Three years passed and Jane had two more children: May and Rosy.

Bringing up a family of six wasn't easy. The National Health Service and social security weren't even thought of then, and having a large family, Jane found her money soon ran out.

'I'll have to get a job, Alfie,' she said.

'Poppycock! No wife of mine is going to work, I'll sort it out,' Alfie replied, determined to find a way to earn more money.

Alfie knew he had to stop drinking if he wanted to support his family. He tried to go without his beer, but found that the more he tried to stop, his mind went back to the war and he couldn't sleep. He suffered with shell shock, and the only way he could deal with it was with alcohol.

Jane eventually got a part-time job in a fish and chip shop. This worked out well, because she took home for her family the food that didn't sell at the end of the day.

Beth and May were at school, but Hettie stayed home to take care of Rosy. Jane was educated, so she taught her children how to read and write in her spare time.

There were times when Hettie had to show her face in school, because it was against the law not to go.

Emma Cross was Jane's friend and neighbour, and she kept an eye on Rosy when no one was with her.

Sometimes Rosy was left with her comfort blanket and the door open.

'Emma! I'm off, see you later,' Jane would say, knocking on the door of her friend's house.

'Where'd yer leave her, Janey?' Emma said.

'She's playing in the hallway.'

'All right, I'll be over in a minute.'

Most of the time Emma looked after both Hettie and Rosy, but Hettie was very independent and responsible for an eight-year-old.

'Hettie! Where are you off to?' said Mrs Potter, her teacher.

She was a huge woman with a chest as big as two large melons. Her face was round with rosy cheeks. She had a stern look on her face, but there was a kind of warmth to her that made the big woman become a gentle giant.

Folding her arms, she said in a low, deep voice, 'It's only half past ten! You have another two hours before it's dinner break.'

The teacher knew very well where the girl was going. Hettie usually got away without her noticing.

'Sorry, Mrs Potter, I have to get back to Rosy – she's on her own,' Hettie said, feeling a little nervous of her teacher's reaction, as she was making her way towards the door.

Mrs Potter called after her as she ran out the door, 'I'll have to report you to the school board!'

Hettie wasn't worried about that. She only had one thing in her mind: her little sister, Rosy.

She ran down the road as fast as her little legs could carry her and almost knocked down an old man with his walking stick.

'Sorry, Mr Page!'

I hope Rosy is with Mrs Cross, Hettie thought, running into the house and calling for Rosy.

'Rosy! Where are yer?' she shouted, with tears welling up in her eyes. 'Where are yer, Rosy?' Hettie was looking everywhere, frightened that her baby sister had gone missing.

'Rosy!'

'She's here with me!' Emma called from over the road. 'Don't worry, your mum hasn't been gone long. Rosy's playing in the back garden with Ronny.'

Emma had two children. Ronny was three and Ruby was six. She had had twins, but they died four years ago with the consumption, when they were only a year old.

Thank God for Emma Cross, Hettie thought. It was a shame about her husband, though; he'd lost his leg in the war.

Emma earned enough to keep them comfortable. She was a seamstress. The clothes that were worn during those years had a lot of workmanship in them. The local fashion shops gave her plenty of work, doing alterations.

Beth, who was six years old, had her mother's fine mannerisms. She said, 'Mummy, I'm going to wear beautiful dresses like Aunty Em makes when I grow up.'

'I'm sure you will, Beth. You'll grow up to be a beautiful princess and marry a prince,' Jane said to her daughter.

Beth believed this, and went about with her head up high and making out she was a princess.

She was always dressing up in her mother's clothes and wearing her shoes, parading up and down the street. If you wanted to find Beth when she went missing, you only had to look in the wardrobe.

The poor people bought most of their clothes in the market – 'Petticoat Lane', they called it. All sorts of goods were sold and bought that way.

Emma was known to help the poor by altering the clothes to

fit them. She was always ready to help the down-and-out.

She was a lovely lady, a bit on the chubby side, but a happy soul, considering the disasters she had in her life.

Jane's oldest child, Freddie, was fourteen and hardly ever went to school. He earned money at a young age to help his mother. He was a newspaper boy, selling papers on street corners.

He got to hear about the world news first; for instance, Albert Einstein won the Nobel Prize for physics and mathematics. The flying Smith brothers won £10,000 for the first flight from Britain to Australia, in under thirty days.

'Read all about it! Einstein marries second cousin Elsa! Read all about it!' he'd shout.

He was a short kid, with a flat hat (known as a cheese cutter), cord pants, a short grey jacket, long grey socks and brown shoes.

Freddie hung about with the men who gambled in the streets; he kept an eye open for the cops and ran errands.

He was a boy who would do anything to make money for the family. If anyone wanted anything, Freddie would get it.

He had contacts with the people in the right places, so to speak. Most of the men that looked after Freddie did so because they feared his father. They didn't want to get into his bad books.

'Six! Come on!' Rolling the dice, Alfie said, 'Yes! Double six!'

There were eight men betting odds against evens.

'Throw it again, Alfie,' said the taller man. Alfie shook the dice in the palms of his hands, giving them a lucky blow, then he threw them against the wall.

'Yes! Twos, double twos!' Alfie yelled out excitedly. He kept this up for a while. Then young Freddie joined them.

' 'Ello, son. Did yer get those bags over to Mrs Green's?' Alfie said, as his son threw the dice again.

'Yeah, and I've sorted out the horse.'

Freddie helped out with the deliveries at weekends. He was black with the coal dust.

'Three and a two.'

'Not so lucky this time, Alfie,' said one of the men.

'C'mon, Dad, show 'em how to do it! Take all their bloody money,' Freddie said with a cocky attitude.

'Cheeky bugger! Yer wanna take him in hand – or I'll will!'

said a short fellow with a cigarette hanging out the corner of his mouth.

'What's that yer said, mate? You'll do what?' Alfie stood up and pushed the man against the wall. 'Do yer want some of this?' Alfie held his knife close to his face.

'OK, Alf. Jesus, man, yer don't have to get nasty! I'm not spoiling for a fight.' The man was shaken with Alfie's sudden action.

Alfie released him. 'Keep yer mouth shut if yer know what's good for yer.' He picked up his winnings and said to his son, 'C'mon, Freddie, let's get yer home, it's getting late. Yer muvver'll be wondering where yer are, and we don't want 'er rabbitin' on again 'bout yer working at the yard and getting yerself dirty.'

After the war, Alfie became a violent man. He took on anyone who challenged him. Many times you'd see him fighting in the street, stripped to the waist with his fists up.

He was proud to show off the scars that he got from the war. He became a feared man in his neighbourhood; even the police were afraid to go down the road where he lived.

Campbell Road was known as the worst road in London. They called it 'The bunk' (or Campbell bunk).

The men gambled in the streets, not caring one bit that gambling was illegal.

Lou, she was her father's favourite. She was strong and tall and got the nickname 'Long Lou'. She had a fiery temper just like her father. She was the only one of the family who stood up to him. She could twist him around her little finger. If it weren't for Lou, her father would have done far more harm then he did. He loved his daughter and didn't want her to be disappointed in him. So, thanks to Lou's manipulation, Jane (most of the time) was able to get what she needed from her husband.

Lou took on too much for her age; she felt responsible for her younger sisters while Jane was working.

She took care of the washing and the cleaning and did most of the ironing. She used a heavy iron that was heated on the cooking range. There were two irons; one was heating while the other was being used for ironing.

The men wore stiff tight collars that did up with a stud and were detached from the shirt so they could be washed and starched separately.

On Sundays the children wore their Sunday best. The girls wore aprons with pleats around the edges. Their boots had buttons that went high up to the leg. They had three-quarter-length dresses with pantaloons. Coats were short with plenty of material.

Jane was proud of her family, and she did the girls' hair in ringlets tied up with coloured ribbons. They walked proudly down the road to church every Sunday, except Alfie; he was in the pub as usual.

One day, a school board man came knocking on the door.

'Is Mrs Jones in?' he said to Lou, who opened the door to him.

'No, she's at work. Who are you?' He was a large man with a moustache, holding his bowler hat in his hand.

'I'm here to speak to Mr and Mrs Jones. It's about young Hettie,' he said. Then he gave Lou an envelope. 'Give this letter to your mother, if you please, young miss.'

Lou took the envelope and giggled a bit. She thought it rather funny being called 'miss'.

After closing the door, Lou did a fancy walk, swinging her hips from side to side and saying, 'Miss Jones, la-di-da!' Lou was a bit of a laugh at times.

When Jane came home from work, Lou said, ' 'Ere, Mum, this came for yer, some gent came from the school board; it's about Hettie not being at school.'

'Oh, dear!' said Jane, after reading the letter. 'It says here, if Hettie doesn't attend school in the future, I will be summoned to go to court, and will be heavily fined.'

'What a load of old tommy rot!' Alfie said. 'Take no notice; he'd better not come round 'ere while I'm about – I'll knock his block off.'

After that warning, Hettie had to go to school. But she was always worried about Rosy being left on her own.

Jane worked hard to being up her family and was proud of her home. The house they lived in had two rooms downstairs. In the kitchen was an old cast iron kitchen range. It had a round lid that opened on the top so you could put the wood or coal in to heat the cooker. Alfie supplied the fuel, being a coalman. The kettle was heated on the top of the cooking range.

There were gas mantles on the wall. Candles were used at night. In the back scullery there was a boiler. This was known as a copper. It was made to have a fire underneath to heat the water. The washing was done in the copper boiler. The large sink had a scrubbing board in it, and next to the sink was a mangle.

The toilet was in the back yard and had a wooden seat.

There was a tin bath hanging on the brick wall of the house. Bath night was always on Fridays. The little ones were washed in the copper boiler.

The front room had an oak table with six chairs, and under the window was a small table with sides that dropped down. It had an aspidistra plant on the top. A piano stood in the other corner of the room.

Jane was very proud of her best room and kept it well polished.

Upstairs there were three bedrooms. Hettie, Beth and May were in one. Freddie shared with Lou, and Rosy was in with Jane and Alfie.

Under the bed was a jerry that was used at night because it was too cold to go outside to the toilet in the back yard.

In winter, it was so cold at night that sleeping together was the best way to keep warm.

The house was always full with Freddie and Lou's friends. Jane was happy with a house full. But there were many times when she was exhausted with all the worry and hard work she endured. She often prayed to God to help her and take care of Rosy.

Hettie overheard her mother's prayers one night and thought she was asking God to take Rosy away. This scared her, so she got on her knees and prayed, holding her little hands together and saying, 'Oh, please God, don't take Rosy! I'll take care of her, don't listen to Mummy, God, she doesn't mean it.' She felt responsible for Rosy and loved her dearly. 'Please, please, God, don't take Rosy away!'

As time went by, baby Rosy became sick with the measles, and then she got pneumonia. She died just before her second birthday.

The day before Rosy was buried, she lay in her little coffin in the best room on the oak table. It was too sad to keep the coffin lid open, so the family and neighbours said their goodbyes by giving the little coffin a kiss.

Young Hettie was in such a state that she cried, 'Mum, Dad, please don't put Rosy in the ground! She's afraid to be on her own.' Her tears were falling down her little face and she was sobbing her little heart out.

Lou and Freddie were holding back the tears, trying to be brave, because they knew how hard it was for their mother and father. They didn't want to make it any harder on them by showing their pain. So they held their chin up the best they could.

The other two, Beth and May, were too young to understand what death was. They just kept quiet and stayed with Emma Cross most of the time.

Finally the day came to bury Rosy. Her small coffin was lifted from the table by her father and placed very gently in the horse and carriage hearse.

That was the first time anyone saw Alfie with tears falling down his face.

There were so many flowers you could hardly see her little white coffin. Over a hundred people were at Rosy's funeral. You could hear the sobs from outside the church.

After the service, Rosy was buried.

Hettie felt so much pain in her little heart, and from that day on she made a decision to close her heart to the world, because the hurt was too much for an eight-year-old to bear.

Alfie's sadness took him back to when his brothers were killed in the war. He became a bitter man and drowned himself in alcohol.

Hettie couldn't come to terms with Rosy's death, even though she was a strong character, the kind of child who was the leader of the gang so to speak, a caretaker to all the down-and-out kids.

Sometimes she would round up all her friends and go to Rosy's grave, hoping and praying that Rosy would be there, waiting for her.

Lou would always know where to find her if she went missing. 'Come on, Et, let's go home,' she would say.

Lou was her big sister, and Hettie would hold her hand and go home, looking over her shoulder and thinking, Maybe tomorrow Rosy will be there…

Alfie's drinking became too much for Jane. They were always fighting. She was so bruised and battered.

Then, one day, Alfie came home drunk and picked a fight with her. He grabbed her long hair and swung her around the room. Then he violently swept the mantelshelf clear with his arm, making everything fall onto the floor.

Freddie tried to stand up to him, but he was too small and young to do anything to help; he just got thrown across the room, splitting his head open on the brass fender. He managed to get up, with blood running down his face.

'Get off her!' he cried out hitting as hard as he could at his father.

Hettie was hiding behind the door, holding onto Beth and May. It frightened them so much they went running across the road, calling out to Emma Cross, 'Help! Dad's killing Mum!'

All the neighbours came to their door, shaking their heads in disgust. 'They're at it again,' they'd say.

Just then, Lou came around the corner. She was on her way home from work. When she saw the commotion, she started running down the road.

'Oh, no, not again!' she groaned. She ran into the house and got between the two of them.

'Dad, Dad, stop it! Leave her alone!' Lou shouted.

When Alfie heard Lou's voice, he looked startled as if he suddenly realised what he was doing. He was in one of his blackouts due to too much drinking. He wasn't in his right mind.

'Get away from her!' Lou said and pushed him out.

Alfie fell out of the doorway and went staggering down the road. He spotted the onlookers on the other side of the road.

'What you looking at? Want some of this?' he yelled, holding his fists up in a threatening attitude. 'Go on, you noisy lot! Bugger off before I knock yer blocks off!' He growled.

Inside the house, Lou and Freddie started picking up the broken bits off the floor. Beth, Hettie and May were still hiding in Emma Cross's house.

'What a mess, Mum,' said Lou.

'Why do yer let him in when his drunk? Yer know what he's like!'

'I didn't see him… he saw me as I was passing by the pub. I said "hello" to Lenny Harris. He said I was messing around with him, and then he followed me home, shouting at me!' Jane sobbed, with tears falling down her face.

'He'll be back tomorrow hoping to make it up with you, so don't let him in.'

Lou was right. He came around the next day with a bunch of flowers and a look on his face that was all too familiar to Jane. But this time she didn't take him back, even though she loved him very much. She just knew it was no good; he would never change while he drank, and she knew he couldn't stop.

I didn't understand at that time that my mother was talking about her own childhood experiences.

I loved to hear about all the drama and was full of questions. I was into the why and what fors.

'Why did Baby Rosy die?' I asked. I was far too young to understand what death meant. 'Is baby Rosy in heaven now, Mum?'

'Yes, we will all see her again one day. Now, c'mon, Kate – up to bed!'

My mother gave a big sigh; I could see some tears in her eyes.

'Don't cry, Mummy! Rosy will be waiting for you in heaven,' I said.

My mother closed her eyes for a moment then wiped her tears; then Billy and my sister Rosy came in.

'You still up, Kate?' Rosy said.

'What's the time?'

'It's just gone eight, Mum.'

'Oh, dear, I got carried away…'

I was sent to bed.

'Good night, Mum.'

'Goodnight, Kate, sleep tight.'

I was thinking about my father and was longing for him to come home. I didn't know him at all, because he left and went overseas when I was six months old.

~5~

In the morning we got up for the Saturday morning pictures.

'Here's a shilling each. Now don't forget to take care of Katie,' my mother said to Rosy and Billy.

I was nearly five now and loved going to Saturday morning pictures with my siblings. We all ran to the bus stop.

There was a phone box next to the bus stop that we kids raced to get to, because sometimes there was a tuppence left in the telephone box that the last person left behind. If we found tuppence we'd go by bus; if not, we'd walk.

The picture house was called the 'Rink'. It was in Finsbury Park.

All the kids started off with a song: *'We come along on Saturday morning, greeting everybody with a smile,'* and so on.

Usually the cartoons came on first, e.g. *Roadrunner, Donald Duck,* and *Bugs Bunny,* with his famous expression, 'What's up, doc?'

The kids got so excited when Rin-Tin-Tin came on. They let all their steam out by stamping their feet on the ground, shouting 'Hooray' to the goodies and hissing to the baddies.

Superman and *Roy Rogers,* with his horse, Trigger, were my favourites. At the end, Bugs Bunny came on and said, 'That's all, folks.'

Afterward we went to the pie and mash shop for a bowl of mash and liquor. This was our Saturday treat.

Aunt May was staying with us while she was pregnant, so my mother was busy taking care of her welfare.

'How yer feeling today, May?'

'Bit sick.'

'Think you had better tell the doctor and get a check-up, see if the baby's OK.'

'Yeah, I will, I'll go first thing Monday morning.'

'You need to find out when the baby's due.'

Six months later, Aunt May was a bit down. She was heavily pregnant and was afraid of what her husband, Jack, would say about the baby. She didn't know that my mother had already written to him, telling him everything. She was like that, a proper controller.

'Oh, come on, May; let's go to the flicker to cheer you up. Charlie Chaplin's on at the Rink.'

'Oh, all right, Et, I could do wiv a bit of cheering up.'

That evening we all went to see *The Tramp* (the first movie Chaplin made). He was a shabby but fastidious man. He was known for his sad, lonely whimsical manner with a spirit that couldn't be destroyed. Just the tonic Aunt May needed. She laughed so much, that when she got home her waters broke and went into labour.

In February 1945, four days before my fifth birthday, Aunt May gave birth to a baby boy. He was born perfect.

Aunt May was ecstatic; at last she had her baby, and I was so excited to have a baby in the house.

'Can I hold him, Mum?'

Aunt May let me hold her newborn baby; he was adorable.

Aunt Lou came to visit.

'Watcher, Lou! Ain't he lovely?' said May, holding her baby in her arms for her big sister to approve of.

Lou looked at the newborn and said, 'Mmm – he's gorgeous! Is he all right, May – you know, ain't nothing wrong wiv him?'

'Doctors said he's fine.'

'That's great!'

Lou gave her sister a kiss, and a loving smile.

'Now, you take care of him and don't let anyone push yer into doing anything you don't want to, OK!' Lou said with a protective attitude.

'Has Mum seen him yet?'

'No, she's coming this afternoon; Beth's bringing her. I think I'll call him Johnny. What do you think, Et?'

'That's a good name, May. Yeah, I like it: Johnny, mmm.'

'What do you think Jack will say?'

'Don't worry about that now. He'll probably love him when he sees him. I'll help yer find a place of yer own, near me, May.'

'Thanks, Et.'

Aunt May found a flat in the next road to us and was always in our house. Johnny became like a baby brother to me.

Two months later, the end of the war in Europe was in sight. Germany's towns and cities were subject to some of the most devastating air raids of the war. The Red Army took control in the ruined streets of Berlin. Then, on 30 April, Hitler committed suicide; he shot himself. Field Marshal Keitel signed Germany's unconditional surrender on the 9 May. It meant victory, and peace in Europe was at last secure. The war was over!

'Et, it's over! The war, it's over!' May yelled and jumped about with tears in her eyes. We were all so excited. All the people came out in the streets, hugging one another.

The next day, Mum said, 'C'mon, May, let's go to the West End.' Everyone was so excited. 'Rosy, Billy, get yer coats on! We're going to the Palace.'

'Will we see the King, Mum?' I said.

'Yes, and the Queen,' my mother replied, full of excitement.

We all went to Trafalgar Square.

The Prime Minister Winston Churchill broadcast on loud-speakers, announcing the official end to war with Germany and declaring a public holiday: VE day (Victory in Europe).

The atmosphere was electrifying. My mother, Aunt May and us kids joined the crowds outside Buckingham Palace, which became the centre for much of the celebrations.

The people cheered when the King, Queen and the Princesses, Elizabeth and Margaret, appeared on the balcony of the Palace.

The King and Queen waved to the crowds, while Churchill and the two Princesses smiled and waved.

'Look, Kate, the King and Queen are waving to you!' my mother said.

I was lifted up to see the royal family and the Prime Minister.

We were told that in the evening the Princesses left the Palace to join in the celebrations. Then we made our way down to the Mall to join the crowds in Piccadilly. Floodlights illuminated the cross on St Paul's Cathedral; it was a sight to remember.

All that week there were street parties for the children, with flags, decoration and paper hats. Our street organised the tables in a V-shape.

'Will my daddy come home now?' I said.

'Of course he will, Kate, soon.'

It took another three months before my father came home.

Jack came home first. Johnny was three months old when Jack first saw him.

His train from Waterloo was due in at 10.30 a.m. They were so excited.

May didn't know what to expect from him; her mind was in a right state. 'What if he doesn't want me, Et?' she said.

'Don't worry.' Mum put her arms around her. 'If he loves yer he will forgive yer.'

'What's the time, Et?' Aunt May said biting her nails with worry.

'It's only half past nine. Now look here, May, if he don't want the baby, I'll keep him.'

'Thanks, Et. I dunno what I would 'ave done wivout yer!'

The train pulled in at Waterloo station on time. We all stood on the platform eager to see my uncle Jack get off the train.

'There he is, Et!'

Among the many soldiers and sailors, there was Jack, with his big army sack on his shoulder and his soldier's hat covering his fair hair.

When he saw May running towards him, he dropped his sack, took off his hat and made his way towards her. May flew into his arms and they kissed and held each other. His blue eyes filled up.

'May, my darling wife, I have missed you so much!'

'Oh, Jack, my darling, it's been so long. I'm so sorry…'

'Hush, May, don't say anything.'

He understood that life was lived a day at a time during the war. We didn't know if there would be a tomorrow.

When Jack held baby Johnny in his arms, his heart melted and he loved him as his own son from that moment on.

~6~

My mother got a job working in Lyon's Corner House, a self-service café in Holloway Road. She was a nipper.

I went to a nursery. Rosy picked me up after school. Billy took himself home.

Sometimes my mother worked late, so I was left with Rosy and Billy. They looked after me and gave me my tea. Bread in hot milk was on the menu in those days.

I was at the mercy of my siblings. Many times I was made to eat when I didn't want to.

Rosy and Billy were out to please their mother, because she was very controlling and put the fear of God in them if they misbehaved. If the place wasn't clean and tidy when she came home, they'd be in for it. We all experienced the broom chasing us down the stairs when we were on the run from her anger.

One day Billy had an idea.

'Come 'ere, Kate, put the dusters on yer feet,' he said. 'You too, Rosy.'

It was a sight to see the three of us having fun skating up and down polishing the floor with dusters tied around our feet!

We got up to all sorts of mischief when we were left on our own.

One time we thought there was a burglar in the house, upstairs in the bedroom.

It scared the life out of me.

'You go first, Billy!'

'No, you.'

Then they both looked at me and said, '*Kate!*'

I was under their power and did as I was told.

' 'Ere, hold this knife and go upstairs... we will be right behind you!'

I can remember to this day the scene of Billy and Rosy behind me, scaring the life out of each other. I crept up the dark stairway and slowly opened the bedroom door.

'Can you see anyone, Kate?' They sent me in first.

'No, there ain't no one 'ere.'

They sighed with relief.

When my mother came home, I told her what they did, sending me upstairs with a knife in my hand. She gave them a good telling off for frightening me.

'Get to bed, the three of yer, and behave yourselves.'

The next day my mother was home early.

'What yer got for dinner, Mum?' Billy said.

'Lamb stew.'

'Can we go out to play for a while, Mum, until dinner's ready?' Rosy said.

'OK, but don't go far, be in at nine the latest.'

She put the wireless on, and to her astonishment she heard her name being announced. 'Hettie Wallis, your husband will be here to speak to you on air tomorrow at four in the afternoon; be sure to be by your wireless.'

'Oh, my goodness!' my mother said, putting her hand to her mouth, surprised to hear her name mentioned. A few minutes later, there was a knock, knock! on the door. Aunt May called through the letterbox, 'Et, you there?'

The door was opened and in came Aunt May, blurting out, 'Did you—?'

'Yes, May, I did,' said Mum, interrupting her sister.

'Oh, Et, that's smashing!'

The next day, Nanny, Beth and Harry turned up with their two children. Then came Lou with her boys, and Aunt May and Jack with baby Johnny. The whole family gathered around the wireless and waited in anticipation for the broadcaster to say my mother's name again. Then the announcer said, 'Good afternoon, people, this is *Forces Favourites*. Are you there, Hettie? We have your husband, Eddie Wallis, here. He has a message especially for you.'

Then my father's voice came through the speakers of the wireless.

'Hello, my darling, I hope you are OK. I miss you so much. Say hello to the kids and all the family. I love you very much.'

'Is there anything else you want to say, Ed?' asked the announcer.

'Just keep smiling, love, I'll be home soon.'

'We hope you got that message, Hettie.' That was all, he was gone. The broadcaster then said, 'Tomorrow we have someone special for Mary Conners. Be sure to be by your wireless, Mary, same time tomorrow… Now we have a song for all those waiting for their sweethearts and husbands to come home.'

The song they played was, *'We'll meet again, don't know where, don't know when, but I know we'll met again some sunny day.'* It was one of Vera Lynn's songs. The whole family joined in with tears running down their cheeks.

The weeks went by, and still no news about my father coming home.

'Mum, will you tell me a story tonight?' I asked.

'Well, all right, Kate. Would you like something to eat first?'

'Yes, please, can I have a sugar sandwich?'

My mother made me a sugar sandwich and a cup of orange juice, made from the concentrated orange juice that the USA supplied for the children. It was part of the lend-lease agreement.

It was a warm evening in July; the sun was shinning through the kitchen window. Rosy and Billy were out playing with their friends, as usual.

My mother made herself a cup of tea and then said, 'Are you comfortable, Kate?'

'Mmm,' I said, licking the sugar off my hands.

'Well, then, I'll begin. Once upon a time…'

~7~

Young Hettie, who was just turning twelve, was riding her bike, trying not to get the wheels caught in the tramlines. She was on her way to her father's coal yard.

'Dad, I'm here!'

Alfie was covered in coal dust, with an old rag in his hand, wiping his face.

He wore an open-neck shirt with a scarf around his neck, sleeves rolled up above his elbows, and black trousers held up with a black belt and a brass buckle.

On his head was a flat cap that he lifted to wipe his forehead. He was still a handsome man.

'Watcher, cock!' he said when he saw his young daughter. 'You're a sight for sore eyes.' His smiling eyes covered up the deep sadness that was inside him.

Alfie still loved his wife and children and missed being with them. He knew his drinking was at the heart of the matter, but the drink came first in his life, not to mention the gambling.

'Can I have a ride in your cart, Dad?' Hettie said.

' 'Course yer can, duck, I've just fed Mo.'

Alfie took his young daughter around the back of the yard to the stable where he kept the coal.

There was old Mo, his faithful old mare, still attached to the cart. Hettie climbed up. Her father led the old mare around the stable on the cobbled ground. 'Don't get yerself dirty, or yer mum will be after me,' Alfie said.

'I won't, Dad.'

This was a real treat for Hettie. She missed her father and looked forward to the weekends when she hired a bike to get some housekeeping money from him.

'How's Lou?' he asked.

'Oh, you know, Dad, she still won't talk to yer,' replied Hettie. 'She's got a bloke, his name's Sam; think he wants to marry her, Dad.'

'What? Over my dead body!' Alfie said. 'I'll sort him out.' His face turned angry. 'I'll give her getting married – she only fifteen, the little floozy!'

Lou was coming up to sixteen, and had been seeing Sam for three months. He didn't know how nasty her dad was until he came across him outside the pub one night.

'What's this I 'ear 'bout you wantin' to marry me daughter? She's only a minor! If I 'ear that you've been taken liberties wiv her, ye're in for it, do you savvy, you no-good little brat!' Alfie had the young boy by the throat, almost choking the lad.

When Lou got to hear about what happened, she went storming to her father's coal yard.

'Dad!' Lou shouted. 'What the hell do you think you're doing? I've never been so humiliated in all me life! Sam's my boyfriend, so leave 'im alone.' She was furious at her father.

'But Lou, ye're only fifteen...'

'It's none of yer business! If I'm old enough to look after your kids, and work to keep meself, I'm old enough to have a boyfriend. So keep yer nose out, and don't come round the house any more – ye're not wanted!'

Her words cut through Alfie like a knife. He kept away after that. But poor Sam was always looking over his shoulder after the rollicking Alfie gave him.

As time went by, Alfie got involved with another woman, but no one would ever take the place of his Janey, she was the love of his life. Jane felt the same.

Jane's heart was broken when she found out about the other woman in Alfie's life.

A few years later, he sold his coal delivery business. He moved to Ramsgate with his new mistress and started a B&B business. Lou made sure that none of the family saw him again.

Jane took refuge in her family. Her house was full of Freddie and Lou's friends. Every weekend she brought a jug of beer from the pub, and young Freddie played the piano with his pint on the top, playing the old favourites.

The family and friends sang along together: 'Knees up, Mother Brown', 'Roll out the barrel', and 'Toot toot tootsie goodbye'. They all enjoyed a good singalong. Jane never felt alone. The love in the family was her comfort and support.

Lou was going out with Sam for years, then along came Ted. She married Ted six months after meeting him.

Sam's heart was broken. He was too much of a gentleman and looked to Lou for support, whereas Ted was a man who Lou needed. He had a strong will and made Lou feel that she could lean on him.

Young Freddie, on the other hand, didn't get involved with a girl when he was young. He had many admirers, but didn't have time to stay around long enough to be steady. He worked in the newspaper business. The editor of the *Market* newspaper gave him a job as a journalist.

He hung about with gangsters a lot and was involved with high-powered businessmen. That's how he got most of the inside information he needed in order to write about how the money market was doing.

Beth, she was the smartest. She was full of herself, always fixing her hair. She had kiss curls on each side of her face.

A proper little Miss Prim, she loved to dress up. She married her childhood sweetheart, Harry, when they were only sixteen.

Harry's mother was against them getting married. She said they were too young. Every time Beth and Harry went to the church to call out the banns, she put a stop to it. They eventually got away with it by using a forged signature on the consent form.

Harry's mother didn't know that the reason they were in such a hurry was because Beth was pregnant.

May met Jack at the Palace dance hall. She was a happy girl, always laughing. You couldn't tell that she was a bit slow learning. She would repeat herself over and over again. She called herself the ugly one of the family. Jack was a quiet man, and he fell for May because she was loving and kind. She didn't have a bad bone in her body. Jack was very patient with her. I guess he could see her golden heart. May was like a child, she was as innocent as the day she was born. They were made for each other, and were married in a church with four bridesmaids. It was the happiest day of May's life.

Hettie was now coming up to seventeen. She had her mother's green bewitching eyes, her father's smile and black hair.

Her life was full of fun. She had many friends and a few admirers. She gave them all the runaround – until she met Edward.

Eddie wasn't one of the local boys; he lived in Highgate. He was working in the decorating trade with his uncle.

He was riding a bike on his way to a job in the area, when he collided with Hettie riding her old bike. He had a new bike and was showing off, riding with no hands. Hettie wobbled and nearly fell off.

'Watch it!' she said.

He didn't apologise, but just insulted her bike. 'That's a bit of old iron! Why don't yer get off and push it?'

'Don't be cheeky!' she answered back. 'You get off your bike and push it, you ignorant snob!' Hettie was so angry she shouted out, 'Stupid snob!'

Eddie stopped and turned around, and when he saw what a looker she was he wished he'd kept his mouth shut. He was sorry he insulted her bike, even though it was a bit of a wreck.

'I'm sorry I didn't mean to hurt your feelings. Look, you can have a ride on my bike if you like.'

'Get lost,' Hettie said.

'Don't be like that!' Eddie was thinking fast. Erm, how can I get this gorgeous girl to pay attention to me? I know, I've got a bar of chocolate in my pocket.

This was the very thing that Hettie would be interested in, as she didn't get many luxuries.

'Here, have my chocolate,' said Eddie. He put his hand in his pocket and pulled out a bar of milk chocolate. 'I'm really sorry... What's your name? My name is Eddie. I live with my uncle in Highgate. Where do you live? If you like, I'll ride with you to your house.'

Hettie's anger soon died when she saw the chocolate, but she had too much pride to let it go that easy. Besides, the last thing she wanted was to let this boy see where she lived. She could see he came from a good home. Highgate: that was in the country, she thought. Maybe he lives in one of those best houses where all the snobs live. Still, she did think he was rather handsome. She swallowed her pride and said, 'Well, all right then, I forgive yer.

My name's Hettie, and I don't need any of yer chocolate, thank you.' What did I say that for? she thought. I would love some of that mouth-watering chocolate, I must be barmy...

'Pleased to meet you, Hettie. Here, have some chocolate.' He broke a piece off from the bar and offered it to her.

'Well, OK, just a little bit, and you can call me 'Et'. Everyone does.'

Hettie put the chocolate in her mouth. Oh, it tasted so good! But she didn't let him see how much she enjoyed it.

'I ain't seen you about 'ere before. What yer doing around 'ere, then?' she said with a straight face, making out she was hard. But underneath all the charade she was a little excited about this new boy in town. He was so good-looking, with dark brown eyes and lashes that swept right up to his brow. He had a lovely smile. Hettie felt her knees go a little weak, or could it have being the fright she'd just had? Nevertheless, she was smitten with this boy. But she wasn't going to let him see how she felt, not yet anyway.

Eddie spoilt Hettie. He bought her many presents, silk stockings and scarves; the latest style dresses and shoes, perfume and many flowers. He took her dancing and to the flicks to see Al Jolson in his first talking movie.

Hettie loved dancing the Charleston. This was the new dance that came from South Carolina; it was all the rage then. She enjoyed every minute of the attention she was getting.

Eddie was so in love with her. He waited two years for her to slow down. Then he asked her to marry him. She turned him down. She wasn't ready for marriage yet and she wanted to have fun. The truth of the matter was, she was afraid to let her defences down.

Eddie got very upset at the way Hettie played him about, so he decided to join the Royal Navy.

That's when she knew how much she loved him; she missed him far more than she realised she would. She knew then that he was the only one for her. He was away for three months. She thought she'd lost him.

Then one day, one of her friends said, 'Et, there's a sailor looking for yer.'

'Where?' she said, with a skip in her heart.

'He's at your house.'

Hettie ran all the way home, hoping it was Eddie. When she got to the corner of her road she stopped and gathered herself together, and wet her fingers to straighten out her kiss curls. She stood up straight, chin up, shoulders back, and started to walk down the road as if she wasn't bothered.

Meanwhile, Eddie came out of the house and started to walk towards her. Her heart began to beat faster when she saw him in his navy uniform. He looked the most handsome man that she had ever seen. Her footsteps quickened, and then she broke into a run, straight into his arms. They kissed and held each other. Eddie swept her off her feet, lifting her up and swinging her around.

'Darling,' he said, 'I tried to get you out of my head, but I love you too much.' He got down on one knee and said, 'Hettie Jones, will you marry me?' Then he gave her the most beautiful ring she'd had ever seen.

Hettie had tears in her eyes; she thought she had lost him. She took the ring and said, ' 'Course I'll marry you.'

They embraced, and the look of love Eddie had in his eyes said it all. He loved her so much.

They married six months later.

Hettie's wedding gown was made of lace, along with her head veil. She looked wonderful. Ruby, her best friend, and May were bridesmaids.

~8~

'Come on now, Kate, and you two,' my mother said, looking at Rosy and Billy. 'It's time for your supper.'

We all tucked into some lamb stew.

'Get yourselves to bed now, it's nearly nine.'

She was all out of stories and put the kettle on to make some tea. As for me, my head was full of wedding bells and pretty dresses...

Following VE day, the war continued for a further three months, until Japan surrendered on the 14 August 1945. On 6 August an atom bomb was dropped on Hiroshima, and three days later a second atom bomb was dropped on Nagasaki.

The devastation of that action shocked the world. A very high price was paid to put an end to the war. All those lives were lost. This was the price paid to save lives, as the war with Japan could have gone on for many more years. All that was waiting was the official surrender by Japan to put a final end to the war. All in all, the war lasted six years, all but twenty days.

Once again there were celebrations in Piccadilly for VJ day (Victory over Japan). They went on all night long.

The men were at last coming home. My father was one of the soldiers who were in the Far East with Allied forces, the Americans and Australians, fighting the Japanese.

When all the soldiers came home they didn't have any civilian clothes to wear because they were in service all through the war. The government gave them all ration books, identity cards and they were entitled to one suit, one raincoat, a shirt, two pairs of socks, a collar and a pair of shoes.

At last my father was on his way home. My mother made sure everything was in order at home. She wanted her husband to see that she had done well to keep a home together for him to come home to. She even bought an old second-hand piano. My father played a little.

Aunt May went with my mother to Waterloo Station to meet him while us kids stayed at home, waiting.

I was five now and was so excited about meeting my father for the first time.

Aunt May told us later what happened that morning when my dad got off the train and saw my mother for the first time in years.

'The crowd was gathered around the platform, the atmosphere was full of apprehension. Wives, mothers, children and sweethearts were all waiting for the return of their loved ones. I saw him first,' Aunt May said. 'I knocked your mum with my elbow. "There, Et, he's just got off the train, about halfway down the platform," I said.

'Your mum was a little taken aback when she saw only a shadow of the man that she knew. He looked so small and old. Nevertheless she was glad to see him again. She made her way towards him and said, "Ed! Ed!" There he was standing before her. They held each other for a moment, and then your dad kissed her. Both of them had tears rolling down their cheeks. Your mum said at last, "You're home."

'Your father had changed so much. Your mum whispered to me, "He has false teeth and his hair's receding – he feels like a stranger to me."

'Your dad looked at your mum and I could tell he saw the same wonderful girl that he had left behind. He was so glad to be home.

' "The kids can't wait to see yer, Ed, let's get a taxi home," said your mum.'

The front door opened Rosy and Billy went scooting down the stairs.

'Wait for me!' I shouted.

I was going as fast as my five-year-old legs could go one step at a time. When I finally reached the door I saw my father for the first time. He was cuddling Rosy. Billy stood back. Then he looked down at me. His first words to me were, 'She's not mine, is she?' It was a fact that I was his daughter, although I had to wonder if he had his doubts.

It didn't go as I visualised. He didn't pick me up in his arms. He didn't even kiss me. I felt disappointed and thought, what's the matter with me? I'm so small, I'm grubby. My hair's too straight. I'm not good enough, he doesn't like me.

None of this was true, of course. I was a strong and sturdy girl and had the most beautiful eyes; my lashes were thick and long. I had short black hair with a fringe. My voice was a little husky, which was quite cute. All in all, I was a very beautiful child. But I didn't know it. Billy wasn't able to show his feelings. He was a bit of an introvert. He didn't look too happy when his father came home. He was used to being the man about the house. It took him a long time to accept his father. He hated the smell of smoke from his cigarettes.

'He smells, Mum!' he said. But after my father bought him a bike, that did it; he felt better and slowly built up a bond with him.

I never got the love from my father that I needed to validate me. He never, in all my life, sat me on his knee and said he loved me. This was the beginning of my low self-esteem. I spent the rest of my life looking for the love that should have been given to me from my father. I had no idea that from that day forward I became a lost child.

One day I asked my mother, 'Mum, why doesn't Dad love me like he does Rosy?'

'It's only natural for the firstborn to be the favourite,' Mum replied.

Well, that didn't help. I became confused and thought, It's because I was born on Friday the 13th that I'm unlucky.

One afternoon, I said to my mother, 'Mum, yer know, yer haven't told me any stories for a long time.'

She looked at the clock and saw she had some spare time. My father was at work; he was a bus conductor.

'Come on, then.'

She made a cup of tea and sat down in her usual armchair.

'Are you comfortable, Kate?'

'Mmm,' I said, holding my much-loved china doll with the eyes that opened and closed.

'Then I will begin. Once upon a time…'

~9~

Eddie was still in the navy, so Hettie was out and about with her friend Ruby. They loved going to the pictures.

The silent movies came to an end in 1929, when for the first time all-talking and all-singing movies were showing.

The magic of Hollywood's golden age was on the horizon. The most magical time was just beginning.

Hettie and Ruby didn't have a care in the world – until Hettie got pregnant. She was twenty-one.

Hettie wasn't very good at childbirth. She was two days in labour when she had Rosy. She didn't want to be born, so they had to pull her out with forceps.

At first they thought she was stillborn. It took a good few minutes to get her to take her first breath.

Hettie was so weak she actually had an out-of-body experience. She was looking down on herself. She said she would have gone out of the window if it had been open.

Dr Barnes told Hettie, 'Now listen here, young lady, you mustn't have any more children.' The doctor then turned to Eddie.

'Do you understand, Mr Wallis? I strongly advise you not to have any more children. Hettie has a curved spine which prevents her from having a normal delivery.'

'OK,' Eddie said. He was so grateful that the doctor had saved his wife and child, and he said, 'I'll be careful.'

Eddie wanted to be with his wife and child after the traumatic delivery. But being in the navy, he had to wait until his leave before he could get home. He had six more years to serve.

He tried everything to get out of the navy. Eventually he got a discharge on the grounds that his wife had postnatal depression and was anaemic.

He was a good father to Rosy; he absolutely adored her, and he dressed her in pretty clothes and showed her off to all the neighbours, he was so proud of his beautiful daughter.

Rosy was a pretty child. Her eyes were deep blue – you would think they were purple – and she had the sweetest smile. One would never guess that she was very difficult to cope with. She'd scream and stamp until she got her own way. She had quite a temper. Hettie thought she might have been affected by her birth trauma.

Britain was in a depression when Rosy was born, as was most of the world. Two million Britons were out of work, and the dole money was only 29s 3d.

Germany had five million unemployed. They looked to Adolf Hitler's Nazi party to solve their problems.

In 1929 the stock exchange on Wall Street in America collapsed. The market plummeted. Their hopes were on a presidential candidate, Franklin Roosevelt.

Like most men in the early 1930s, Eddie had a hard time finding work. He tried being a salesman, going from door to door selling tea. His real trade was painting and decorating, but not many people had the money for luxuries like that then.

Hettie got a part-time job working in a battery factory while Eddie looked after Rosy.

Two years passed, then Hettie became pregnant again.

There weren't any birth control pills during those years. Legal abortion wasn't heard of. Although women won the right to vote, there was still a lot of sexual discrimination and male chauvinism going on.

It took another thirty years before women held their own and became equal to the male dominance over women.

Hettie, being a tough lady, put the fear of childbirth in the back of her mind. Eddie, on the other hand, was very concerned and a little afraid. He didn't want to lose her; she meant everything to him.

Billy was born in the summer of 1934. He was named after his great-uncle, who was killed in the First World War.

Bringing Billy into the world took a long time. Hettie was very weak after she gave birth to him. She was hours in labour.

Eddie was pacing back and forth, smoking his Player's cigarettes.

'Do you think she'll be all right, May?' he asked.

'Don't worry, Ed, you know what a strong lady she is,' May said, biting her nails, worried sick.

Rosy was with Beth and Granny. Hettie had been in labour for twelve hours, and was having a tough time.

A few more hours passed and then Eddie heard the midwife say, 'It's coming! Come on, Et, you can do it, push! I can see the head. Push, Et!'

Eddie felt so anxious. He got down on his knees and prayed. 'Oh, God please take care of my Hettie; help bring our baby into the world safely.'

Then there was a loud, deep, cry that sounded as if it came from her whole body.

'It's coming! Push, it's coming! He's here!' the midwife cried, relieved that it was all over.

Once again, the doctor warned them not to have any more children.

'You have too much of a hard time bringing babies into the world. Don't have any more, please, Hettie.'

Eddie came into the bedroom and kissed his wife.

'It's a boy, then.'

Hettie smiled and said, 'Is he all right?'

Eddie looked at the tiny, screwed up face. He was sleeping.

'Look's OK to me, mate.' He smiled at his wife and said, 'Well done, we have a son.'

Six years passed, and Hettie fell pregnant again. She didn't want any more children, so she did all she could to get rid of it. She tried jumping down the stairs and taking cod liver oil. It worked; she had a miscarriage, only to find that she was pregnant again soon after.

Kathleen was born on 13 February 1940.

'Quick, Rosy, get your father – the baby's coming!'

Rosy ran all the way to Fonthill Road, where her father was a stoker in the Great Western Laundry. In she ran.

'Dad! Baby's coming!'

Eddie put down his shovel, wiped his hands and face, got his overcoat and hat and said, 'Oh, no! Not to day – it's the 13th!'

Eddie was a superstitious man. Friday the 13th, he believed, was unlucky. He wouldn't even go out on that day. He said to Hettie, just before Kathleen was born, 'Don't have the baby on the 13th, whatever you do.'

'I'll get the doctor, Rosy. You go back and look after yer mum.'

He lit a cigarette and then made his way to the doctor's surgery.

May was so looking forward to this baby being born. She couldn't have children herself. Being a bit on the simple side, May took it into her head that Hettie didn't want this baby because of her miscarriage she had before Kathleen was conceived. So she thought Hettie would let her keep her. She waited patiently outside the door until the baby was born.

Ten hours later, Kathleen was born – on the 13th. It wasn't a Friday, but for some reason or other, Kathleen was led to believe that she was born on a Friday. No one knows why this was so.

At least the delivery went well. May was so excited, she held the baby as if she were her own.

They say that if a baby is conceived in love it has more of a chance to survive and do well in life. Well, if that was true, Kathleen was in trouble. But the love that came from May's heart was a welcoming gift that Kathleen needed. Kathleen may not have been conceived in love, but she was received with love from her caring and genuinely kind Auntie May.

Eddie took one look at her and said, 'Not another girl!'

Hettie was just happy that it was all over.

'Watcher gonna call 'er, Et?' May said.

'Kathleen.' It was her mother's middle name.

'Can I call her Kate, Et?'

' 'Course yer can.'

'Kate… I like that, don't you, Ed?'

Hettie looked over at Eddie and he said, 'Whatever – I don't mind.'

He looked down at the baby and gave a little smile, thinking, She looks all right. He was relieved that she was OK.

'Well, I better be getting back to work now. Can't slack, what with another mouth to feed,' he said, relieved it was all over, and feeling pleased with himself that all had gone well and the baby was fine.

May took Kate everywhere with her. She bought her clothes and gave her all the tender care she needed. Eddie didn't take much notice of her; he had to work all hours to keep the family together.

It was then that I realised my mother was telling me the story about my own birth.

'Mum, I wasn't really unlucky, because everything went well, didn't it?' I said.

' 'Course you're not unlucky, Katie, that was just your father's silly ways.'

Maybe you could have seen it as being unlucky, the year I was born – not in the sense of my father's superstition, but in the timing of my birth.

The Prime Minister, Neville Chamberlain, had announced on 30 September 1939, 'This country is at war with Germany.' A month later on 1 January, two million nineteen- to twenty-seven-year-olds were called up.

On 9 April 1940, a full-scale German invasion of Norway began. Denmark had already been overrun. It was 14 June 1940 when Hitler invaded Paris and took over.

The King asked Neville Chamberlain to resign and asked Winston Churchill to form a new government. On 10 May, Winston Churchill became Britain's Prime Minister. His first speech in the chamber of the House of Commons included the words, 'I have nothing to offer, but blood, toil, tears and sweat.'

On 18 August, Luftwaffe pilots homed in on Southern England. The Battle of Britain began.

On 15 November in Warsaw, 350,000 Jews were confined in a ghetto. The most horrific feature of the Second World War was the Holocaust – the destruction of life on a massive scale. The persecution of the Jews was undeniably one of the most shameful actions in human history.

On 29 December 1940, London had the biggest air raid of the war. The Luftwaffe pilots razed one third of the city, including the Barbican. Luckily, St Paul's survived among the flames. The

Blitz started in September 1941, killing about 13,000 citizens and wounding thousands more.

My father joined the army, much to my mother's disgust; to think that he could leave her on her own to take care of three children while a war was on…

He came to say goodbye, but she was so upset that she made sure she was out with the children.

He left a wind-up gramophone with a record by Vera Lynn: 'Keep on Smiling'. She didn't see him again until the war was over.

~10~

It was Friday night: bath night.

'Kate, time for your bath.' My mother brought in the tin bath from the back yard. She heated the water in a couple of buckets on the top of the gas cooker.

Rosy and Billy went to the public baths. One could get a lovely hot bath there for fourpence.

Beth took her washing there. It was very handy for the people who didn't have a bathroom. Only the best houses had bathrooms in those days.

There was a fire going with the old tin bath in front. The oven door was left open with the gas full on to heat the room. My mother was so used to bathing us kids this way. Carrying the hot water from the cooker and pouring it in the bath was quite a skill. When the water got a bit cold, she'd say to me, 'Mind yourself.'

Then she would pour the hot water from the kettle in the bath while I was still in it. I had to get out of the way pretty fast. My mother didn't pussyfoot around, or mess with her words. If she said jump, you had better jump. She wasn't a tactile woman; she didn't kiss you, ever, or give you a loving hug, but she took responsibility for her family and was a good mother. She made sure her children were well fed and warm.

On a cold night, she'd give us a hot-water bottle, in the form of a glass lemonade bottle. How they never cracked when she poured in the hot water, I will never know.

I wrapped myself up in bed, trying to warm myself with the hot lemonade bottle. My feet were the hardest to get warm. I'd get my feet warm first, and then cuddled the bottle. Sometimes it was too hot to touch, so I'd warm the cold sheets by my feet, until the bottle was just cool enough to touch. My mother put coats on top of the blanket for extra warmth. My nose and ears got so cold in the winter I'd bury myself under the clothes until I fell asleep.

We kids played outside most of the time; I was allowed to play in the streets at five years old.

My playmate lived opposite; her name was Maureen, nicknamed 'Midge'. It was a love–hate relationship. The street was our playground. We'd hang a rope around the lamp post, sit on it and swing from side to side, never tiring. Sometimes the grown-ups had a rope going across the road and we'd play skipping. The grown-ups had a go at times.

One day I decided to go travelling and went to visit my nanny.

I travelled with my mother to her house many times, so I could remember the way. It was about a fifteen-minute walk to her house. I had to cross a main road, but there weren't many cars about then.

When I got to my nanny's house, Aunt Beth opened the door. Surprised to see me, she said, 'What are you doing here, Kate? Are you by yourself?'

'Mmm, I've come to see Nanny.'

'You're a clever girl to travel all this way by yourself,' Aunt Beth said, holding her new baby, Christine, who was six months old.

'Hello, Nanny,' I said, feeling so proud of myself for my achievement.

'Hello, sweetheart!' my nanny said. 'Did you come on your own?'

'Yes, I knewed the way all by meself, now.'

She gave me a hug and said, 'Well done.'

She wasn't well, she had been ill for some time. I was unaware that I wasn't going to see my nanny for much longer. She had cancer.

'You be careful going home, now, Katie.'

She was standing by the gas cooker that was on the landing, putting the kettle on.

I will always remember her that way: my nanny wearing a long grey flannelette dress. She looked so weary. She passed away six months later.

I had all the wonderful memories of her life in the stories that my mother told me.

It was 1947. I was in the infants' school, just across the road from where I lived.

One day my teacher said, 'Next term, children, you will be

moving up to the next year and you will sit in alphabetical order.'

I didn't know my alphabet and was afraid to tell the teacher, so I asked my mother, 'Mum, will you help me to learn my alphabet?'

'Ask your father,' she said.

'Dad, will you help me learn my alphabet?'

He replied in the same old sarcastic nature. 'You can't learn anything; you're just like May – stupid. You're probably end up marrying a dustman.'

I was used to the nasty remarks that came from him. I didn't answer him back. I knew by now it would only make matters worse if I cheeked him.

I decided to teach myself. I had a little red money box that had the alphabet on it, and I can remember reading the letters repeating them over and over again until I taught myself the A B C that morning. That was the way it was for me; I had to figure things out for myself.

The forties were the beginning of the great Hollywood days and all the family enjoyed the pictures. We went at least one a week, sometimes twice.

The MGM studios became the lead producer of musicals featuring actors such as Frank Sinatra, Doris Day, Mario Lanza and Judy Garland. The dancers on screen were Fred Astaire, Ginger Rogers and Gene Kelly, and many others. It was the most exciting time ever for the world to lose themselves in love and romance.

The Hollywood movies took me out of reality. My favourites were the romantic musicals. It was an opportunity for my fantasies of love and romance to take flight.

I was at an impressionable age – seven; I had no sense of reality, I thought life was about what was portrayed in the movie world, not being able to understand it was all just entertainment.

During the war, many Hollywood stars had travelled overseas to support the troops fighting for our country. The wonderful songs of Vera Lynn included 'There'll be Bluebirds over the White Cliffs of Dover' and 'We'll Meet Again'.

Thank you, God, for the music.

On cold nights, walking home from the pictures, my mother

bought hot chips wrapped in newspaper.

Yes, they were good memories.

On Sunday mornings I was sent to Sunday school. I loved Sunday school, it was a real treat. I loved to listen to the stories about Jesus.

The storyteller said, 'Jesus loves you, he died on the cross for you.' I became interested the moment I heard, 'He loves you'. Being only seven going on eight, I believed everything I heard, especially if it was about love and kindness.

I wasn't aware that I was starved of love and affection. I may have had security at home, and my parents did love me, but it wasn't enough; something was missing. I didn't know what it was at that time.

Then I heard the Sunday school teacher say, 'If you give your heart to Jesus, he will come into your heart and be with you always.'

Well, that was all I needed to hear: 'be with me'. I will give my heart to Jesus, I thought. He said he loves me. So I said to myself, 'Jesus, will you come into my heart?'

I didn't feel any different, but I believed in all the stories about God and the Lord Jesus, and listened to the teacher when she spoke about wisdom. She said that it was worth more than silver and gold, and when you prayed for what you want, God would answer. So I thought, I'm gonna ask for wisdom and strength. Yes, that's what I want to be, wise and strong. Little did I know what I was setting myself up for with that request!

Maybe there was a change in my life after I prayed for Jesus to come into my heart, because I felt a little more understanding towards my father.

The thing to do is turn the other cheek, I thought. That's what Jesus said.

I attended Sunday school every week, and loved to colour the pictures of Jesus and his disciples. I collected all the little texts with proverbs on and received a Bible for good attendance. I treasured my little prize.

Sunday was a good day when I was a child. The traditional Sunday roast aroma greeted me, along with Billy playing his favourite records, such as Frankie Lane singing 'High Noon'. The kitchen window was wide open for all the neighbours to hear.

Sometimes Billy went to Chapel Street Market on a Sunday morning to buy records. One Sunday when I came home from church, I heard a sound coming from the cooker. 'Mum, what's that noise I can hear?'

'Daddy brought home some chicks from the market. They're on the on top of the grill, keeping them warm.'

My mother showed these tiny baby chicks to me.

'Can I hold one?'

'Be careful, then.' She gave me one to hold in my hand.

'Ah, ain't they lovely! When they get big, will they lay eggs, Mum?'

'Yes, and then we can eat fresh eggs every day.'

We also kept rabbits in the garden. They weren't pets; my mother kept them only for food. When they were big and fat enough she'd get Mr Kichener to kill them. He lived around the corner. He also killed the chickens for our Christmas dinner. All my aunts had one for Christmas Day dinner.

Rabbit stews were often on the menu, so were pig's trotters, pig's head and tripe.

Christmas was a time for presents and parties. The paper chains were handmade. Some were glued and some were sewn. I was good at sewing. I didn't learn very much at school, but sewing was my gift.

I'd gather the crêpe paper together on the sewing machine, and then twist them around making a colourful paper chain.

Rosy turned the handle of the little Singer sewing machine, while I did the gathering. It was a real family time, decorating the Christmas tree and wrapping presents. It was my job to wind up the gramophone when we sang Christmas carols.

I always had a doll for Christmas.

Christmas Eve was so exciting I couldn't sleep.

In the evening all the family walked to Aunt Lou's house for the Christmas party.

My cousins and I stayed in the house, while the grown-ups went to the pub. My mother never stayed overnight, no matter what the time was. She'd gather up her children like a mother hen and walk home, rain or snow. They were the good times.

I was still getting emotional abuse from my father. He never had a good word to say about me. One day I said to my mother, 'Mum, why is Dad so nasty to me?'

'Well, Kate, when your father was born, his mother didn't want him and his sister. She abandoned them when they were babies. Your dad's father's name was Bert Wallis. He looked after his children the best he could. But being an entertainer, he couldn't take proper care of them.

'Bert was well known at the seaside resorts singing and playing the piano. He wore a straw hat and wrote songs. He called himself "Bert Dale". Some of his songs were sold for sixpence. One of those songs got to be well known. ("For the love light of your eyes and the sunshine of your smile.") They played it sometimes on the wireless.

'He had many admirers, but the women who went out with him soon got fed up with his children. He left them with his girlfriends for days, sometimes weeks, without any financial support. So your father and his sister, May, often went hungry. Sometimes they were locked in the cellar and ate raw potatoes because they were starving.

'Your granddad couldn't cope with the two of them, so he took May back to her mother. Eventually, she put her in an orphanage.

'Your dad stayed with his father until he was fourteen. Then he took him to his uncle in Highgate, where he was taught the decorating trade. He never saw him again. He stayed there until he joined the Royal Navy.

'There's an old saying,' my mother added: ' "The measure of love that we are given can only be the same measure of love we can give and the same measure of love we can receive." '

My father had anger and resentment towards his parents because they abandoned him. He hadn't dealt with it. It was still deep inside of him. From time to time he'd vent it out on those he was nearest to. I was the one he used.

He loved his wife and was afraid of rejection from her; the same with Rosy. All I knew was it was very damaging to me psychologically.

I learned later in life that my mother had shut down her

feelings because of the trauma she went through when she lost her baby sister, Rosy. She closed her heart that day.

Both my parents had been emotionally unavailable, and being the third child and not wanted didn't help matters.

On top of that, my father's superstition about Friday the 13th was another issue I was up against. I was affected far more than I could handle.

It was different with Rosy; she was a love child, and the fact that Billy was a boy, gave him the right to be born.

Fortunately, spending the first three years of my life in the country was a blessing. Living close to nature feeds the spirit. For we are, after all, 'human nature' – we are apart of creation. Therefore we are connected to the wonder of all that is.

I must have harmonised with the sound of birds singing in the countryside. I drank milk straight from the cow and ate freshly laid eggs. Therefore I wasn't a completely hopeless case.

The breeze rustling through the trees sounded as if nature was singing a lullaby to me when I was left in my pram for so long while my mother worked.

The quite evenings and the love of the neighbours sharing their home-grown fruit and vegetables was a good start in life for me.

Things changed when my mother went back to London. Now came the raids, the blackouts, the shortage of food and the fear on my mother's face.

At four years old I didn't understand what war was all about. I was told once, 'Life is like a white tablecloth; some stains don't wash out.'

~11~

In January 1950 Danny was born. He was the child my parents decided to have because they missed five years with the others, due to the war.

'Can I hold him, Mum?' I said. He was so tiny, a gorgeous baby. I was ten now, and Danny was a blessing in my life. I watched over him like a guardian angel. I loved him dearly.

At that time Rosy was working as a secretary in a printing factory. Her boss, Mr Turner, known as Mr T, didn't have children of his own. Rosy became the child he didn't have. He took her everywhere and taught her how to become a hard-headed businesswoman.

All this went to her head. She'd come home preaching to the family about life and how you should treat others. The next thing you know this Mr T was running the show, so to speak.

He showed off his big American Cadillac car. The family was in the grips of a super male chauvinist. He called himself 'God'. He had power all right – the entire family was in awe of him.

I was invisible when this man was around. Even Rosy got on the bandwagon and spoke to me as if I was a big mistake.

He changed the family lifestyle profoundly. He showed my mother and father a lifestyle that normally would have been out of their reach. There was dining in restaurants, going to a film star ball, getting dressed up in long gowns with orchids pinned on their shoulders. I looked on and I really, really wanted to go.

'One day we'll take you, Katie,' my mother said.

I longed for that day to come. I was the one who stayed home babysitting Danny. But no fairy godmother came to my rescue.

Two years passed, and I was at secondary school now.

'Katie, come on, move yerself, you'll be late!' called my mother.

I was tired because Danny had wet my bed again. He was put in my bed at five every morning.

My mother went off early in the morning, cleaning. Nine times out of ten, Danny wet my bed.

'Ugh! He's done it again!' I cried.

'What?' my father said.

'Danny – my vest is soaking!'

'Wait till your mother comes home.' He was too busy getting ready for work to deal with it.

As soon as my mother came home my father left. They were like ships passing in the night. I took care of Danny until my mother took over.

I got myself ready for school.

'Don't forget to put on your bodice, Katie.'

I wore one of those bodices that did up with little rubber buttons, a white blouse and a navy pinafore dress. This was my school uniform.

'Have you got your beret?' my mother called out, as I was putting on my blazer by the front door.

'Yes. I'm going now, Mum. See you dinner time.'

My school was over a mile away. By the time I'd walked home for lunch, and then back again, I'd walked about five miles. I did this daily and hated walking to school because my shoes were worn down, with holes in the soles. It didn't help much with cardboard insoles. My feet got so cold, and if it rained, I'd have wet socks.

Many times I wore my plimsolls. The cold was unbearable at times. I often came home with my toes, nose and fingers so cold; I got what you'd call 'hot heat'. This was a burning that was really painful. My mother put my hands under running cold water to help bring them back to the correct temperature. It was a horrible experience.

My father tried to repair my shoes with cheap bits of leather, but the nails sometimes were a little too long. I'd feel them sticking into my toes. It hurt so much I'd take my shoes off and changed into my plimsolls.

At school, I felt as if I was on the outside of life, looking in through a glass partition. Something wasn't right; I was a lonely child, leaning up against the wall in the playground on my own, wondering why I felt so different from the other kids. I felt a bit like a lost child.

Most of my childhood was spent around my family. If we didn't go to the pictures, we'd visit my aunts.

Aunt Beth one evening, then Aunt Lou the next.

Aunt May was always in the house with Johnny; he was a pain in the arse sometimes, a right handful.

Aunt Lou always baked some cakes as soon as we arrived. She was a character. I loved to visit her. I'd sit on a stool by the fireside being quiet because we were told children should be seen and not heard. I was instructed not to ask for anything.

Aunt Lou kicked off her shoes and twiddled her toes in front of the fire and said, 'Well, what do yer know?' Then the gossip would begin.

Every year the whole family went to Ramsgate. It was our favourite seaside resort. Aunt Beth rented a house for all the family.

One time I asked if I could bring my friend, Midge, along.

'OK, Kate, just as long as you behave yourself,' my father said.

Billy's mate, Roy, came; Rosy brought her friend, Rita.

In the evening, we all went to a place called the Arena.

Midge and I played around the penny slot machines with some pennies in our pockets. I tried to win a cigarette for my father. I'd put the penny in the slot, flip the lever and the ball had to go into the correct space to win. I was delighted when I won a cigarette and went running to my father to give him my prize, hoping for some kindness from him for my good intentions.

Nothing. I didn't get one word of praise. In fact, he must have thought it was good to keep me under his power by being harsh on me. I wasn't prepared for what happened that evening.

There was a band and an entertainer who invited the holiday-makers up from the floor to give a turn on the stage. This particular night, Midge got up. I was fascinated by her courage and sat myself in front of the stage, watching with admiration, when suddenly, *smack!* I was slapped hard across my face. I was shocked, because all I was doing was looking at my friend.

'Ouch! What was that for?' I held my hand on my face with tears welling up in my eyes. 'What did I do?'

My father didn't say anything. He just walked away without any explanation. I went running to my mother.

'Mum, why did Dad hit me – and in front of all those people?'

She didn't show any support whatsoever, but she did say, 'That's what you get for being jealous of Midge.'

From that day on I wanted to run away from the confusion of my dysfunctional family. I'd daydream about being married and having my own family.

In reality, I was looking for someone to mend my broken heart and love me.

I had trouble learning at school. I listened to the teachers and tried so hard to concentrate and understand what they were teaching. I couldn't comprehend very much. It was as if my mind had closed.

Maybe it was part of nature protecting me from the false information that was being impregnated into my mind by all the outside negativity that was going on in my life.

I read somewhere that the universe works in mysterious ways; it doesn't judge the thoughts that you think, it just obeys them. So every thought, every statement, and every feeling is creative to the degree that it is fervently held as truth; to that degree, it will manifest in one's experience. In other words, we're not what we think we are, but we are what we think. We are the creators of our own reality.

I was unaware that I was making a self-fulfilling prophecy. I fervently believed the things my father told me as I was growing up, for instance, 'You can't learn anything'. Therefore I found it hard to comprehend my lessons.

~12~

It was Saturday morning.

'Kate, when are yer getting up? I want you to collect the bag wash. Come on now!' My mother was shouting at me again as if I was deaf.

Rosy was still asleep. She was allowed to sleep in because she worked and paid her way.

My parents wanted to go into the pub business. They had tasted the flavour of money, now they were taken over by so-called 'God'. They started training for a while. I'd looked after Danny two nights a week.

'What time will you be back, Mum?' I said.

'Just after eleven, you'll be fast asleep by then.'

Danny and I were in the house on our own. Billy was doing national service and was sent to Germany. Rosy was always out.

I hated being alone; I couldn't sleep until my parents came home. I'd lie there for hours listening for their footsteps to come. Danny was in his bed fast asleep. I'd lie in bed listening for their footsteps. The night-time was scary and my imagination went wild.

Then I thought I heard a sound that came from downstairs. I froze with fear and waited to hear if the noise came again. It was all quiet.

I then heard footsteps in the distance getting closer and closer. They passed by.

Once again I'd listen out for the next set of footsteps. I listened for hours until the footsteps stopped outside.

They were home at last. My fear subsided immediately.

My mother decided she couldn't keep the training up because Danny was too young to leave and I was only twelve, so they waited a few more years to carry out the dream of owning their own pub.

I guess I wasn't a stranger to fear. I feared the atom bomb, and thought that the world was going to end. That was because of all the talk about the hydrogen bomb.

It all began just after Danny was born, in America.

President Truman ordered the Atomic Energy Commission to produce the hydrogen bomb, so that America could defend itself. He was concerned about the Soviet Union, because they had successfully exploded an atomic bomb four months earlier. I heard all the propaganda and, being only young, I took it all in.

In 1952, King George VI died, on 6 February; but it wasn't until 2 June 1953 that Elizabeth II was crowned. That was a day to remember. I was thirteen; we watched the coronation at Aunt Lou's house on an eight-inch TV set. We sat watching the whole ceremony all day. It was so grand; the gilded carriage drew her though London streets. Elizabeth never imagined that she would inherit the throne because her uncle, Edward VIII, was king, but he abdicated when she was ten years old.

It was a sight to remember. I was so proud of my country that day and became all patriotic. I went about waving a Union Jack flag.

The Queen gave a speech on the radio and said, 'I have my husband, Prince Philip, to support me.' And she thanked people all around the world for their good wishes. The Queen's children, Prince Charles and Princess Anne, who were four and two years old, attended the ceremony.

This was also the year I came close to death.

One night, I didn't feel well. I was rolling around in pain.

'Ed, I think you better get the doctor,' my mother said.

This was about eight in the evening. My father walked to the surgery.

An hour later, Dr Nathan examined me and then said to my mother, 'I'm going to call an ambulance. Kate needs to go into hospital; she has what they call rumbling appendicitis.'

I was taken straight into the operating theatre.

As soon as they opened me up, my appendix burst. I was operated on just in time; I could have died if I'd been left any longer. My father saved my life that night.

I lost a year of schooling, because my recovery wasn't easy; there were complications. That didn't help my education. But I did receive a prize for needlework.

The 1950s are remembered for many things. It was the beginning of a new era, when so many wonderful things stayed in the mind for many years to come.

There was fast food. First Wimpy hamburgers, and now McDonalds has over 30,000 local restaurants in more than one hundred countries. The founder was a man named Ray Kroc.

Jazz, the American music that began around early 1920s in African America, came to Britain.

The typical instruments were the trumpet, guitar, saxophone, double bass, drums, trombone and the clarinet. The words Dixieland, bebop, and the blues covered only a fraction of the style of music that jazz brought about.

The credit card (plastic money) appeared. It was in 1951 when the Diners Club and American Express credit cards were first issued in New York. But it took another ten years before the magnetic stripes were issued.

The creator of this world was only beginning to bring evolution into action when the credit card was designed. No one would have guessed at that time how that small plastic card would engender a mass of globally organised transactions.

Television... I never thought that I would own one! When one did come our way, via the boss man, all I did was watch the Interlude.

The movie stars of the 1950s, such as James Dean, made a mark in history. Unfortunately, he was killed in an automobile accident. He was remembered as a rebel of our times and made the film, *A Rebel without a Cause*.

Then there was the sex symbol, Marilyn Monroe. She was remembered for her 'Happy Birthday' song sung to President Kennedy. It probably didn't do her much good, as she was found dead in the prime of her career. They say she committed suicide, but it was suspected that she may have been murdered.

Rock and roll, with Bill Haley and the Comets, was the best thing that came along for me. I was fifteen years old and loved jiving to their first record, 'Shake, Rattle and Roll'.

I left school in 1955. My first job was in a sweet shop. Being on the shy side, working in a shop helped me to gain some self-esteem.

Mr Harte, my employer, was not sure of me at first.

'Kate, in the mornings I want you to dust all the sweet jars, then the counters. After that, sweep the floor and mop it over.'

'OK, Mr Harte.'

I was very nervous at first, but willing to do my best to please my boss. After a couple of weeks I was on my way to being a convenient shop assistant.

I had fun with the barrow boys who were on the corner just outside. You'd hear them shouting;

'Hearty lettuce, c'mon, mum, get yer hearty lettuce!'

The boys often came into the shop for their cigarettes, and they called me 'darling'.

After a few months, Mr Harte was beginning to trust me and told me that I had a future with him, when I was older.

I told my mother what Mr Harte said about having a future with him.

After that my mother made me leave. She didn't like the idea of me having a future with him. So, reluctantly, I left.

Mr Harte was so sorry to let me go. He said, 'Don't leave, Kate. I will give you a manager's job when you are older. I'm getting another shop. Please don't go.'

He stood in the door way and wouldn't let me pass. 'I'm not going to let you go!' he said with determination.

I cried, I really didn't want to leave. I loved it there, and for the first time in my life, I felt like someone liked me. But I had to do what my mother told me; I was still a child of fifteen, and very much under my mother's influence.

I left and got a job in a children's clothes factory. The manager took to me straight away and got me to do most of the running around for him. I caught on quick and learned the trade in no time.

I was sixteen now, and was going out dancing with my friend, Janet.

'What yer wearing tonight, Jan?' I'd say.

'My black pencil slim skirt and striped top. What you wearing?'

'The same.'

We liked to dress the same.

I permed my hair curly – the 'poodle' style they called it, then.

We girls bought stiletto shoes with heels as high as five inches. Our seamed stocking were 2/6d a pair.

The stockings had to be put on with care, as they easily laddered; the suspender often came undone. We thought nothing of lifting up our skirt and fixing them in front of people, then checking out the seams to see if they were straight.

We were a delight to see, the pair of us walking with small steps in our tight skirts, and stiletto-heeled shoes, sometimes getting them stuck in the pavement!

That was a funny sight to see – a shoe stuck in the crack of the pavement, and one of us going, 'Whoops!' and hopping back to retrieve it.

I earned £2 10s a week and gave my mother half, saved a £1 and kept the rest for my self, which was only 5s. I was saving to go to Spain with Rosy and her boss.

'How much yer got, Kate? Janet said.

'Half a crown. What you got?'

'Two bob.'

'OK, we'll get five fags between us.'

We girls managed to buy five 'Weights' cigarettes and paid 9d to get into the dance hall.

I was at last enjoying my life.

The mental battering was still going on at home, what with 'God' (Rosy's boss), and Rosy, with her high achievement in life and having my nose rubbed in it. Most of the time, I let the talking down go over my head; I was mostly out with my mate, Janet.

I was in my element, creeping around the dance floor with some Teddy boy, the starlights floating around the dance hall reflecting from the glass ball in the centre of the hall – it was all so romantic.

One Friday night I was jiving with Janet.

'Kate, look over there! That bloke's looking at you,' Janet said.

I changed places with Janet so I could get a better look. He was standing by the doorway, leaning against the wall and staring at the girls dancing. I thought, I haven't seen him around here before; he can't be looking at me…

'He fancies you, Kate,' Janet said.

'Nah, not me! It's you he's interested in.'

'Why do you think he's interested in me, Kate, and not you?' said Janet. 'Don't put yourself down! You're lovely, your teeth are very white and even, and your face lights up when you smile.'

That was a wonderful thing to say to your best friend, I thought.

'Thanks, Jan, you're the only one who thinks I'm lovely!'

He was about six foot tall, with dark brown eyes and black hair, slightly curly; it looked wet because of the grease he put on. He was wearing a double-breasted suit and the shoulders on him were very broad. Most boys in those days wore jackets with shoulders that were too large for them, but this bloke was busting with muscles.

Then he came over and interrupted us girls dancing; he caught hold of my hand as I spun around. I was so surprised; he was too good-looking for me, I thought.

I was unaware of how I was changing into a lovely girl. I had my grandmother's bewitching green eyes, and the make-up I wore on my eyelashes made me look something like Twiggy; the famous model, she had a figure just as slim.

I was lost for words and felt very uncomfortable. I wasn't used to being looked at, especially by a man who looked like him.

'What's your name?' he said in a soft deep voice.

'Kate. What's yours?'

'Robert – you can call me Rob.'

'I ain't seen you 'ere before,' I said.

'I've just come out of the army. I've been in Germany for two years,' he replied, smiling at me.

'Oh!' Being only sixteen, and very immature, I went quiet and looked down because I felt a burning sensation in my face. I guess I was blushing. Luckily the lights were low so he didn't notice.

The music stopped. Then a slow song came on. It was Sammy Davis Jr. He was singing 'The Birth of the Blues' – one of my favourites.

'Would you like to dance?' he said.

'Sure,' I said, and walked onto the floor holding his hand. He was a good dancer. To my surprise he started dancing the waltz. I just followed his lead. I was a natural at it. He glided across the room, holding me tightly and firmly as if he didn't want to let me go. He held onto me for the rest of the evening.

Janet raised her eyebrows and gave me a smile, as if to say *Well, well, look at you!* I was very unsure of myself; I'd never dealt with a full-blooded man before. I was much too young to be with him. He must have been twenty-something, if he'd just been demobbed from national service.

He spoke very respectfully to me and asked me where I lived, and if I wouldn't mind if he walked me home. I was taken back at his request.

'Yes, if you like,' I told him.

He walked on the outside of the pavement and didn't stop talking. When we got to the front door he politely said, 'Goodnight.' Then he walked away. I was relieved that he didn't kiss me. It would have been too much for me. It was bad enough dancing close to him. If he'd kissed me I would have died. I'd never been kissed before.

I didn't think I'd hear from him again.

On Monday morning, I went to work.

They were very hot on timekeeping. If you were more than ten minutes late, you were sent home and lost a day's work, and you couldn't get away with it because you had to clock in.

Luckily for me I only lived five minutes away. Many times I ran all the way, leaving it until the last minute.

Mr Hayes was my manager. He always had a smile for me. He helped me to learn how to do the cutting, sorting, overlocking, felting, ironing and running around for him.

'I want to learn how to machine the coats, sir,' I said.

'You're too important for that, I'm training you for other things.'

I didn't argue. I hadn't learned to stand up for myself yet.

The buzzer went at six, and everyone clocked out.

I was walking down the stairs from the factory floor and had the surprise of my life. Robert was at the bottom waiting for me.

'Hello, I didn't expect to see you!' I said.

I was impressed, just to think that he found out where I worked and put himself out to meet me. I also felt good, because all the ladies gave him a second glance. Then gave me a look of envy when they saw he was meeting me. He looked so handsome, wearing a light grey double-breasted suit.

Robert walked me home. He told me that he'd been to my house first, and my mother told him where I worked.

'I was wondering,' he said shyly, 'if you would like to go out with me sometime?'

I couldn't believe my ears! Did he ask me out? I held my head down shyly because I felt myself blush again and didn't want him to see.

'Sure… where?' I said.

'The pictures, maybe. There's a film on at the Odeon that I think you will like.'

'OK. When?'

'Tomorrow night. I'll pick you up at seven, then.'

He was gone. I was well happy that this gorgeous guy had come back for me, but there was a strange feeling inside my stomach. I didn't know what it could be.

Once the word was out that I was going out with a twenty-year-old dreamboat, all hell broke loose. My mother spread the word like wildfire.

'Have you seen Kate's new boyfriend?'

Rosy found it hard to swallow, because she didn't have a boyfriend yet. She'd been out with a few men, but no one steady.

The next day, seven o'clock came around.

He's not coming, I thought. Then the doorbell rang. My stomach had butterflies.

'Hello,' I said. 'I won't be a minute. Would you like to come in and wait? I'll just get my coat.'

'I'll wait here, take your time.' He lit a cigarette and waited at the gate. I put my coat on and saw Rosy looking out of the window; she was hiding behind the curtains. Robert put his arm out for me to take. Off we went, walking down the road with my arm in his as if we were old sweethearts. I felt like a million dollars.

Rosy, who was keen on fashion, let me borrow her purple suit. It was one of her old tailor-made costumes. It had pleats at the back of the jacket from the waist down, with a long straight skirt with a split at the back. I wore stiletto-heeled shoes; my hair was bouncy because I'd rolled it up earlier to give it a lift. I carried my envelope bag under my other arm.

'Would you like anything from the kiosk?' he asked, getting his wallet out when we were in the cinema.

'No, thanks.'

He bought some Piccadilly cigarettes.

'Want one?' I took one, but I'd hardly ever smoked.

'Light?' At the first puff, I coughed my heart up, it was so strong.

'I think you had better not,' he said, taking the cigarette from my hand.

The film wasn't very good – some detective mystery.

I was just happy to be out on my first real date. Robert held my hand most of the time we were together.

He was a bit of a talker, very much into the music world, asking what songs I liked.

'Err, the Platters, they've just released their record, "Only You"... and Frankie Lane, "Your Cheating Heart". Doris Day, "Secret Love"... er, Little Richard, "Lucille"... What about you, Rob?'

'I like country music – Dolly Parton, Johnny Cash and Patsy Cline.'

The date went well, except for one thing: swearing, He used the 'f' word and many more unsavoury words too many times, as far as I was concerned.

Swearing was not allowed in my house. Not even the word 'bloody' was spoke at home. I wasn't used to it, so I was well put off.

We got home at ten thirty. I wasn't sure of myself when he kissed me goodnight. He leant over and looked into my eyes. I felt a sudden rush of heat go to my head. I was blushing again. I thought, He really is smashing. Before I could say another word he pulled me to him and kissed me on the lips.

My first kiss from a man. Then his hand went to my breast. I pulled it away. He looked into my eyes and said, 'Are you a virgin?'

'Yes, and I plan to stay one until I get married!'

He smiled and said, 'I'm sorry, I respect that. I promise you I won't touch you again. Can I take you out Saturday night? I have a proposition for you.'

'OK,' I said, 'see you then. What time will you come?'

'Oh, about six thirty.'

'OK, bye.'

He kissed me again with his hands held up high, just to show me where they were. I felt a lot better now that he said he wouldn't try anything on me any more, and he'd said he respected me. I thought about his 'proposition'. What was he talking about?

The next morning I got up for work. Rosy said, 'How did you get on last night?'

'Really good – he wants to see me again.'

'When?'

'Saturday night.'

'Did you tell him about your holiday, in July?'

'Nah, that's a long way off.'

~13~

Rosy was always on about her holidays with her boss. Last year she went to France.

When she got back she went on and on about how the French lived. She learned a few French words: *bonsoir*, and *la porte*, and *allez-vous en*, which means, 'Get out of the way.' The boss man bought a horn for his Cadillac car; it was very loud and was supposed to be tooting, '*Allez-vous en!*' Talk about show-off!

I was taken in with the idea to go with them one day. It all started when the boss man suggested for me to save up.

'If you save £50, I will take you to Spain next year,' he said.

I was determined to see what it was like to go abroad. Rosy made it sound so exciting. I saved with determination for nine months.

'How much yer got saved, Kate?' my mother said.

'£36.'

'Well done, you'll soon have enough to go to Spain.'

The plan was to go the day after Billy got married. He was engaged to Pamela. They met just before Billy went to do his national service.

She waited for two years for her big day. The wedding was this July.

Saturday evening came; I had my hair in rollers all day. If I didn't roll up my hair it would be in a right mess, as I had thick, straight hair, and it was permed. It went all frizzy when it was washed.

I wore a black pencil slim skirt and a white blouse with leg-of-mutton sleeves. It was the fashion to wear the collar standing up at the back of the neck. It was a warm May evening so I didn't need to wear a coat.

'Hello, Rob. You look nice.'

'So do you, sweetheart. I like your blouse.'

He held out his arm for me to take, and made it obvious he'd be on the outside next to the kerb, as gentlemen do. I smiled.

'I love your smile, Kate! It shows your lovely white teeth and the little dimples in your cheeks.'

I wasn't used to compliments.

Most of the time I felt like the ugly duckling in my family. Now I guess this little ugly duckling was changing into a swan.

'Where are we going?' I asked.

'To the Astoria Theatre in Finsbury Park; there's a new comic on.'

'Good, what's his name?'

'Des O' Connor,' Robert said.

We had seats in the upper circle.

It was a fascinating place to visit. As you walked in the entrance, there was in the middle of the foyer a water fountain trickling into in a mosaic pond. In the pond, goldfish were swimming; they were massive and beautiful. I couldn't take my eyes off them.

'Come on, Kate, the show's about to start,' Robert said.

The theatre décor was designed like an old-time Spanish palace.

Up on the balcony there was a row of miniature houses with the lights on, giving the impression of a Spanish village in the distance. They even had Spanish carpets hanging over the balcony. The starlit ceiling gave the impression you were in the open looking up to the real sky. It was amazing.

Des O' Connor was an up-and-coming star then.

I was gradually letting my defences down. Robert got an ice cream in the interval. Then he said, 'I have a proposition for you.'

To be honest, I wasn't that bright, and didn't know what he meant. I just went along with it and said, 'What's that?'

He said, 'Will you be my steady girlfriend?'

I didn't know how I felt; I just shrugged my shoulders and said, 'OK.'

I was completely innocent as to what he had on his mind. I took everything at face value and believed all what was told to me. I wasn't able to judge what was right or wrong yet. All I wanted in my heart was to find happiness, someone to trust and believe in. I often dreamed of having a family of my own. I imagined a family life that had no favourites. Being brought up in the 'Hollywood days', I had no idea about the real world. I was full of romantic ideas.

When we got home that evening he went to kiss me good-night. He said, 'I won't touch you, Kate; I do respect your wishes.'

After that, I began to put my trust in him and felt safe.

On Sunday morning, Billy was up and about with his father.

They went to Chapel Street Market to buy something rather special: a gramophone and some records to go with it. When they got back, everyone was more interested in playing the new records than what happened on my date.

I had learned to keep my personal life to myself. Boasting didn't work for me. Rosy was the one on the pedestal. I learnt to keep my place.

As time passed, I was seeing Robert a couple of times a week. It was good having someone caring for me. Sometimes I met him at his work in Fleet Street.

He worked for the newspapers. He was what they called a jobber. That meant he was passed from one position to another. One minute his was delivering newspapers to the station, and the next he was with the printers unloading the giant reels of paper. Whatever, it was a well-paid job. I learned later he took minutes in meetings. Robert was quite academic.

I wasn't aware of his dark side yet, until one evening we went to a nightclub in Soho.

We were dancing to Little Richard's song, 'Lucille,' when to my surprise some bloke came up to me and asked me to dance. Suddenly, from out of the blue, Rob pinned him up against the wall, holding his hand on his throat. The poor fellow could hardly breathe. 'Keep your hands off, she's my girl!' he said, with a violent attitude.

The young man ran out of the door like a bullet!

You could have knocked me down with a feather. I couldn't believe it. Rob straightened out his tie and acted as if nothing happened. I felt a little sick inside. I didn't like violence. Robert was beginning to show his true colours. His swearing was one thing, but violence was something else. I wanted to go home.

After that, I wasn't sure of Robert, and in my heart I wanted to end the relationship with him. He was too violent for me, physically and verbally. All he ever talked about was how strong his was and how he could take anyone on. I was beginning to feel afraid of him.

I asked my father for some advice.

'Dad, I don't want to go out with Robert any more, and I don't know how to tell him. What do you think I should say to him?'

He answered, 'You can't give him up now. You've been going out with him for three months, and it's not nice to let him down.'

The message I got from that answer was, 'I want you to stay with him in the hope you leave home.'

I was in a catch-22 situation; I was unhappy at home, yet in my heart knew that Robert wasn't the man for me.

My type was Tony Curtis; he was my fantasy. Every time I saw him in the pictures, my emotions were all over the place. He was drop-dead gorgeous: those eyes and black hair! I adored him. I wanted to be Doris Day, married to Tony Curtis.

Billy's wedding was on the horizon and everyone was making plans. Rosy made the bridesmaids' dresses. There were four bridesmaids, and each had a different coloured dress. It was called a rainbow wedding. I wore yellow.

They all had their fittings, and after a few alterations everything was ready for the big day; then off to Spain.

I had told Robert about my holiday in Spain a few weeks before. He was happy for me to see some of the world... or was he?

One evening when Rob and I were on our way to meet my family at the local working men's club, he said, 'I've just got to pop home, Kate, I've left my wallet on the side.'

He lived with his parents and sister about half an hour's walk from my place. We went inside his house. He lived on the ground floor.

The sitting room was a cosy room with a table that had a wine-coloured candle thread tablecloth. On the table was a tray with a teapot, jug, sugar bowl, two cups and saucers, all ready set for a cup of tea.

There was an armchair next to an open fireplace. No one was at home.

'Want a cup of coffee, Kate?'

'Um, no thanks, Rob. We can't stay long, Mum will wonder

where we are. I told her we'd be there around eight.'

Rob had a strange quietness about him that night. He usually talked until the cows came home. He looked at me in a strange way, then pulled me closer to him and said, 'Katie.' Then he kissed me and whispered in my ear, 'I do love you.'

Next, he peeled off my jacket and kissed me again. I looked into his eyes and saw a kind of softness and gentleness that I hadn't noticed before.

'I've been thinking, Kate,' he said. 'We've been going out now for a while... would you like to get engaged?'

I was taken back; I was just thinking how to end the relationship. But instead found myself answering him from my head, not from my heart. The look in his eyes gave me a feeling that I could trust him at that moment. I didn't think he felt that way towards me. I answered, 'Really, Rob? You want us to get married?'

'In a few years, when you're older.'

Then he pulled me down onto the floor and kissed me passionately. My heart started to beat faster. I wasn't sure if it was fear or passion. I'd never had a proposal of marriage before.

I fell for his charms and was powerless to control my emotions. I was lost in his arms and returned his kisses. He slowly took off my clothes, looking into my eyes, and I felt a rush of passion go though my body that I'd never felt before. There was no way I couldn't push him away, not now. I just let it happen.

He was very gentle with me when we made love.

'Don't worry, Kate, I won't hurt you,' he said, looking into my eyes and watching my face as he took my virginity.

When it sank in what had just happened, my young and innocent mind thought, Now, I'll have to marry him.

I had promised myself that I would only give myself to the man I married and wanted to wait until then. I still had the mind of a child. Robert claimed me to be his woman before I went to Spain, just in case someone else did; that was his motive.

Billy's wedding day arrived at last. It was a happy day for Billy and Pamela; everything went according to plan.

The next day, I was on my way with Rosy, the boss man and his wife, Lillian. We set off for Dover to catch the ferry to Calais, the French port.

Rob said his goodbyes on the night of the wedding. The words he said to me troubled me. 'Don't you fuck about with anyone else! You'd better behave yourself.'

I felt a red light go on in my head; I wasn't very happy at his statement and felt very disturbed. I didn't see the signs of how sick he was. But my inner spirit did. I had such low self-esteem then that I couldn't do anything about it.

The holiday in Spain was a bittersweet experience. The boss was a bully and Rosy was under his thumb.

The first day was the beginning of a stormy time; even the trip across the Channel was rough, and everyone was being seasick.

We stayed in a hotel the night before the crossing, because the ferry was cancelled due to the sea being too rough. The waves were as tall as the rocks in Dover. It was very frightening.

The boss man had a fear of flying, so we drove to Spain through France and over the Pyrenees. It took three days of travelling.

It was fun experiencing the different culture abroad. But the toilets were strange; all they had was a hole in the middle that you'd just stood over, to pee in.

It was a long scary drive on the mountain road. The car was so close to the edge at times, and I was terrified.

Eventually we arrived in a place called Sitges, a coastal holiday resort in Spain.

Two weeks soon passed, but the experiences will always be remembered.

The bullfights were something I never want to see again. It was all so cruel. I had to sit through four bullfights. I was horrified with it all; even the poor horses that the picadors rode got hurt. I kept covering my eyes most of time.

What the Spanish see in the bullfight, bewilders me. When the bull was dead, the matador paraded around the bullring and the spectators cheered and threw flowers. If it was a good clean kill, the matador was given an ear from the bull. Ugh! I'm so glad I'm British.

One evening, boss man and a few of his friends took a trip to some famous Spanish footballer's house.

The place was something out of a dream. We drove along the

driveway towards the entrance. The house was built on the top of a mountain; I'd never been to a place so glamorous in my life, it was like a palace. It looked mystical against the stars in the sky. They were so bright you could see the Milky Way and shooting stars.

The host and hostess were Spanish. The only other language they spoke was French. The boss, of course, spoke a little French, so he translated what was being said.

'Would you like something to drink?'

I smiled and said, 'Yes, please, may I have some orange juice?' Then I remained quiet for the rest of the evening.

Then from out of the blue the most handsome man leant over my shoulder and softly spoke into my ear, in broken English. 'Would you like to take a walk in the garden?'

He was someone out of a dream. Before I could answer, boss man jumped up and said, 'Yes! We'd love to.'

He and everyone else got up and went for a walk in the grounds.

The famous footballer was very interested in me, but no way was boss man going to give him any opportunity to make any advances to me. Just my luck! I wonder what would have happened if I had got some time alone with him. What a different path my life would have taken if he and I formed a relationship. Who knows what life would have been like for me then?

When the holiday came to an end, there was a farewell dinner party in the hotel. I was a favourite among the young Spanish boys. They played their guitars and sang romantic folk songs to me. It was great.

I enjoyed my holiday in Spain.

Boss man was a pain in the arse with his 'know-it-all' attitude, but besides that, we did have fun on the beach. The food was good. The Spanish dancers and their castanets were a treat to see.

The next day we set of home once again over the Pyrenees, holding onto our stomach when the car got too close to the edge.

We travelled to Paris. The plan was to spend the last day in Paris.

It all felt worth while saving for a year when I was on the top of the Eiffel Tower, thinking, Look at me! I'm only sixteen and on top of the world!

We went to a nightclub that evening, The Lido. It was one of the most famous nightclubs in Paris. We were served dinner with champagne.

Then the show began. I could hardly believe my eyes when I saw the most amazing sight. There were about a dozen ladies, dressed in beautiful decorated costumes with very large feathered fans that covered their whole bodies, and they had extremely high headdresses which were also outrageously decorated. When they opened up their fan, they exposed diamonds, dripping down and around their naked breasts. They were known as the Bluebell Girls. It was a bit of a shock, seeing their naked breasts. They were strikingly beautiful. They reminded me of peacocks fanning their magnificent feathers. I didn't know what to think of it all. My eyes nearly popped out of my head.

Boss man laughed at the expression on my face. He kept pouring the champagne into my glass. I drank as if it were lemonade. This was the first time I drank alcohol. It went straight to my head. When I went to stand up, my legs gave in and the room went around. I had to be supported back to the hotel.

The next day I was sick and had a dreadful headache. The boss didn't have any sympathy; in fact he insisted that I had to stay awake while travelling the rest of the journey home.

I will always remember that night because it was the first time I got drunk. At least I did it in style!

I went home with some wonderful memories of my first holiday abroad.

We arrived home very late at night; the Channel crossing was calm this time.

I was tired and went straight to bed, happy to be free from the controlling master who took me. In some ways, so was Rosy; he never let up on her. She wasn't able to go anywhere without his permission.

~14~

The next day Rob came around to see me. I felt more mature somehow. My tanned body gave me a healthy look that was appealing to him.

'You look good; did you have a good time?' he said, as he held me in his arms and kissed me. 'I've missed you, sweetheart.'

I returned his kisses and said, 'Me, too.'

In my heart I still wasn't sure of him. I'd had time to think about what happened that night at his parent's house and felt shame about making love. I felt he betrayed my trust in him.

Robert was seeing me almost every night. He bought me a diamond engagement ring. This got up Rosy's nose and she made my life a nightmare.

We went out most every night, just to get away from all the tension at home. I spent many evenings playing records at Rob's house and going dancing. Robert was a romantic; he was always singing to me.

One time as we were walking home, hand in hand, out of the blue he started singing aloud. It was lovely, something you would see in a musical movie. He was a bit of a romantic at times. He sang, *'Only you, can make this world seem right; only you, can make the future bright; only you, and you alone, can thrill me like you do.'* He sang the song all the way through to the end. I felt a little embarrassed at his sudden outburst, but thought, How sweet. Robert did love me; I was his girl and he wanted everyone to know it.

Although I was falling in love with Robert, there was still something not quiet right with the way I felt.

It was his constant swearing. To give an analogy: if you were listening to an orchestra, then suddenly one of the instruments played off-key, it would spoil the harmony. Swear words did that to me; they didn't belong in my vocabulary.

I tried to tell him how I felt, but to no avail. This was his way of expressing himself, and that was that.

A few weeks after I came home, the handsome man from Spain who lived in the palace came to London looking for me. He went to the boss's office to ask where he could find me, but Rosy told him I had a boyfriend, which was a shame! He was quite a catch. To think he came all the way from Spain just to see me! When I heard about it, I was angry to think that I wasn't given the chance to decide for myself.

Destiny played its part in my life. I was meant to marry Robert. Or, was it the brainwashing idea that I had in my mind – you have to marry the man you made love to?

We celebrated our engagement with a party for family and friends. It was a typical fifties turnout. Babycham was a popular drink with the ladies, and the men liked their pints of beer.

I wore a full flared skirt with a coloured netting petticoat underneath; as I turned when I was jiving, the tops of my black seamed stockings were exposed. This is what we girls did to get the attention of the boys in those days. I had a small waist, so the elastic belt I wore complemented my twenty-inch waistline. My turtleneck sweater was pulled down over my shoulders showing off my long neck.

I decided to have my hair cut short into a DA. That style came from the actress Doris Day. My stiletto shoes were five inches high. I was thoroughly modern for a seventeen-year-old.

Robert wore one of his tailored double-breasted suits. He was very proud of his fiancée that night, showing everyone the diamond engagement ring he bought me.

The gramophone was playing Elvis Presley's 75 rpm records. Elvis was an explosion that hit Britain in 1956. He sold millions of records. Everyone was raving on about him. His first hit song was 'Heartbreak Hotel'. He also featured as an actor; the first film he made was *Love Me Tender*.

The twenty-one-year-old rock and roller got his nickname, 'Elvis the Pelvis', because of the way he performed with his hip shaking.

He became so popular that the entire teenage world was going frantic over him. His hit records were 'Hound Dog', 'Love me Tender' and 'Blue Suede Shoes' to name a few. We had no idea how he would end up. All I know was how lucky we were to have him in our generation.

Robert was a right charmer, and knew just how to get me in the palm of his hands. He'd whisper softly in my ear as we danced, 'You look wonderful tonight. You're the best-looking girl here.'

He tried to respect my wishes about the way I felt about our sexual relationship. He controlled his passions most of the time...

...except this one particular night. He had one drink too many, and got a bit carried away when he was kissing me goodnight in the hallway. Hormones were flying everywhere.

My father did a peeping Tom job that night, and watched us making love. After that he spread the word around that his daughter was some kind of sex maniac.

That stigma stayed with me for years to come. I was labelled as a lover of sex, a distortion of the truth that really hurt me.

Rosy was used to being 'top dog', so to speak. I, having a boyfriend and engaged, was something she didn't like. I don't know why, though, as Rosy had so much going for her. She had the love and adoration of my father.

When she was born he showed so much affection to her. This in time helped her develop into a compliant child; therefore she accomplished a high level of achievement at school.

At sixteen she walked into an office for a secretarial job. Not only did she get the job, she also got the love and affection of her boss, who taught her all he knew about life: how to use her mind, to be assertive and have a strong will. It wasn't any wonder that my parents were proud of Rosy.

Me, well, I was just a factory worker, underweight with little confidence in myself. No wonder when Rosy walked into the room, my father jumped up and gave her his seat. When I walked into the room he'd say, 'Oh, it's you.' I was looked down on as if I was an outsider.

Rosy had everything life could offer. But for some reason or other she didn't like me. Maybe I was an embarrassment to her because I wasn't very clever, like she was. She was without doubt far more attractive than me, not only in her appearance, but her attitude towards life was very exciting.

I often wondered what a man like Robert saw in me. I thought he could have chosen anyone to be his girlfriend. I was unaware of what made me attractive to Robert. I had no idea what he saw in me. I can only think it was because I was young and vulnerable. Robert felt he needed to protect me, being a man who was always trying to prove himself. I made him feel worthwhile; it was good for his ego. Maybe he loved me because I was unspoiled and had an innocent mind. He knew I'd be a good mother for his children and be faithful to him. I was like a faithful old poodle, whereas Rosy was like a cat, cunning, who knew how to survive on her own.

She may have had a full life, partying and travelling, but she was short of someone special in her life. I could only think she didn't like me because I was the one who got the man.

The atmosphere at home, after I got engaged, became very tense. I couldn't understand why there was so much hostility towards me; the whole family was treating me as if I was some kind of harlot. I couldn't understand why. I was so very unhappy living at home. The fights and arguments I had with Rosy got quite ugly at times.

I rapidly lost weight, and went down to six stone.

Then one day I was finding it hard to breathe.

'What's up with you?' Mum said. I tried to say, 'I can't breathe, Mum,' but I was fighting for my breath. No one realised that I was having an asthma attack. I ended up in hospital.

Three doctors examined me closely. They were concerned about my weight loss. Then they came to the conclusion that it was in my best interest to change my environment. The asthma was brought on by stress.

When Robert heard this, he took it upon himself to get a marriage licence. He announced to me while I was still in hospital that we were getting married in two weeks' time. I was too sick to know what was right or wrong for me.

When I came home and told my family our plans, it was like letting a time bomb off.

My father tried everything to stop us getting married. He offered Robert money not to marry me. I couldn't understand it, because one minute I was treated like an alien and felt like I wasn't wanted there, then the next, my father was trying to pay off Robert *not* to marry me. I was so confused that I could only think

Rosy was behind it. I felt at that time she hated me and didn't want me to get married. I had to wonder why. Maybe I'll understand one day. I do know that my welfare wasn't the issue here. There was no way my family had my welfare at heart. I don't think they were bothered about what I did with my life. I certainly knew that I wasn't supported in anything I did; that's the reason why I slipped through the net with my learning difficulties. No one gave a damn about me when I was a child. I was called names because I wasn't able to read and write. I was shamed for it. I thought I must have been born into the wrong family. No one asked me what I wanted. I had to figure it out for myself.

My mother, on the other hand, had no idea why there was so much fuss made about me getting married.

She didn't like the idea that I was getting married in a register office. It was a matter of her pride. A church wedding was important to her.

'Come on, Kate, we're going shopping,' my mother said. She'd seen a wedding dress in a second-hand shop.

'What do yer think, Kate?'

There was this gorgeous wedding dress in the window, priced £3. It was made of lace. 'Go on,' she said, 'try it on.'

I did and it looked lovely.

I was like a lamb being lead to the slaughter.

My mother didn't have a clue why Rosy acted as she did; she couldn't understand what all the palaver was about, but in her heart she knew I was better off away from all the troubles at home.

My mother once told me that Rosy was a difficult child, and put it down to her traumatic birth.

However, my parents weren't about to confront her. They were right under her thumb. She had a lot of power over them. I think it was something to do with the boss man, Mr Turner. He was a wealthy man and had a lot of influence over them.

~15~

It was August 1958. I was 18½ years old when I married Robert. The budget was a bit low for a smart wedding, but I did look lovely that day in my lace second-hand dress. The wedding went well, considering the fuss that was made around the idea. Rosy didn't let it stop her from coming.

Nobody knew what went on behind locked doors. You never would have guessed how dysfunctional my life was at home!

When I signed the register, I must admit, I thought to myself, What have I done? I'm only eighteen… I knew in my heart that I was too young to make life-changing decisions, like getting married. I had so many reservations about Robert. I was too afraid to look at them. I didn't have the foundation at home to grow up enough to make my own decisions in life.

My hopes and visions were to mend my broken heart, but I was drifting down the river of life, not knowing where I was going.

Robert was a twenty-two-year-old man and well experienced with women, and our honeymoon was very romantic. He took me to the coast for a week. We stayed in a hotel in the little holiday resort of Deal. We travelled in Robert's two-seater sports car.

After dinner, Robert said, 'Fancy a stroll outside, Katie? It's a lovely warm evening.'

I got up from the table and took my shawl. It was a little breezy on the coast.

The sea breeze gently swept across my very slim body as we walked hand in hand along the promenade.

Robert pulled me close to him. He held my chin up and then he kissed me gently on my lips. He looked into my eyes and whispered, 'Do you want a drink before we go to bed, Katie?'

I was still feeling uneasy about going to bed with Robert, even though his lovemaking took me to paradise. I didn't say anything, just, 'Mmm,' with my wide smile and green eyes. Robert took that as a 'yes'.

We made our way back to the hotel.

'I'll order from our room,' he said.

We waited for the champagne to arrive before taking a shower.

The hotel was a stone's throw away from the beach, and we had a sea-view room with a small balcony overlooking the ocean.

'Champagne, darling.'

Robert poured out the cold bubbling wine into my glass. It was the perfect setting; it could have been a scene from a movie.

'Thanks,' I said.

Then I went onto the balcony and saw the most beautiful sunset. I stood there holding my glass, waiting for Robert to join me.

The sky looked as if it were on fire with shades of orange, pink and blue, surrounding the sun as it descended below the horizon.

Robert came out from the shower and joined me. We both gazed at the beautiful sunset. 'It's a lovely evening, isn't it, Kate?'

Then turned and looked into my eyes and I looked back into his, and his gorgeous liquid brown eyes were looking right through me. We made a toast. 'Here's to us, Mrs Barlow.'

He took the glass from my hand and kissed me. Then he lifted me up in his arms and carried me to the bedroom. I felt like a child in his strong arms. Robert treated me like a princess that week.

After the honeymoon we went to our flat.

We had found a furnished flat a week before we were married.

The couple who owned the house was getting on a bit and were set in their ways. The flat was a little on the old-fashioned side, with high ceilings and a large fireside surrounded by marble shelving. On each end of the shelf were two large statues; one was a boy and the other a girl.

The curtains were brown velvet that was faded on the edge from the sunlight. There were two big armchairs made from brown leather and a rugged old carpet on parquet flooring.

The bedroom consisted of an old-fashioned bed and two wardrobes to match.

Along the hall was the kitchen, with an old electric cooker, a sink, table and chairs, and a wooden clothes rack that was on a pulley. This hung in front of a window overlooking the back garden. The rent was £1 10s a week (thirty bob).

Robert wasn't bothered where he lived; he just wanted to get on with his life. He did his best to be a good husband and looked after me.

Most of his spare time was spent in the garage he hired. His hobby was rebuilding his sports car. He stripped it down to the chassis, then remodelled it into a custom-built sports car.

Danny often stayed with us, as he got on well with Robert. He was like a father to him.

I was feeling better now that I was away from the turmoil at home; I changed my job because the manager wouldn't let me learn to be a machinist. I left and worked in a dressmaking factory nearby. I was put next to an experienced dressmaker and was given six weeks to learn. Then I was on my own. I was paid for the work I did. Piecework, it was called, but it was more like slave labour. To earn enough to make it worthwhile I had to work very fast. I soon became an experienced dressmaker and earned my keep.

It wasn't long after we were married that Robert started to work late, and sometimes he stayed out all night. The old companion – fear – was on my shoulders again. When Robert said he wasn't coming home, I went into a state of panic. I told him how I felt but he couldn't understand it. He went off to work anyway.

At night my mind was constantly listening out for any unusual sound. When the refrigerator turned itself on and off, I was paralysed with fear. I begged Robert to change his shift, but he couldn't; his job was to get the first print out to the railway stations in the early hours of the morning.

He also enjoyed his freedom at night. There were many opportunities for him to have a drink and mix with some of the worldly women out there in the West End. He liked being a night owl.

The more afraid I became, the more I had asthma. Basically, I was emotionally still a child.

As time passed, Robert started to show his true colours. He

became distant and was mostly in bed, sleeping.

After two years I had the desire to have a baby. I got all maternal when one of the ladies at work brought her newborn baby in the factory.

That evening I said to Robert, 'How about if we had a baby?'

He didn't argue as he wanted a child as well.

I had my first baby girl in 1961. We named her Shelley Jasmine; she was so much like her father, with brown eyes and black hair. I fell in love with my baby girl the first moment I held her.

It wasn't an easy birth. I was in labour for two days. I thought it would never come to an end. Eventually the surgeon took me to the delivery room. He was going to get Shelley out with forceps. I couldn't describe what happened next – it was all a blur. All I can say is, thank God for the epidural treatment that is there for the taking today. I don't think I will ever understand why nature is so harsh in the birth department. I am so glad for the young women who can now choose to have the help of the medical assistance such as the epidural. It sure beats gas and air.

'Mrs Barlow! Mrs Barlow!' I opened my eyes, and the nurse smiled and said, 'You have a girl.'

They put my baby in my arms, and straight away I felt a bonding that was pure and innocent. At last I had true love in my arms! I adored her and loved her unconditionally. I wanted the best for Shelley. I wanted to give her all the love that I didn't get.

All seemed to be going well with Robert and me. He had his car to tinker with, and I had my baby to love and care for.

Robert liked being a father, although he was hardly at home. He was so blown away at being a father he wanted me to have another baby straight away. Luckily for me, it took six months before I fell pregnant again.

1963 was about the time when James Bond hit the screens. Robert was so affected by the actor Sean Connery that he started to fantasise that he was James Bond.

He went about acting out his character. I didn't take it too seriously, as he did look a bit like him anyway, but I didn't know that he was also acting out the sexual charisma Bond had worked on the ladies, behind my back.

~16~

Then a big change was about to happen. The landlord of the flat we were living in suddenly died. His wife wanted to sell up. She said, 'I'm sorry, dear, but now that Gerard has gone, this house is too big for me on my own. I'm going to sell it. So, my dear, I have to ask you to find somewhere else to live.'

We didn't have anywhere to go and we had no money. Robert was a big spender. He never thought of the future, he lived for the day and was in debt.

Not many landlords were happy to have a baby in their house. I had no where else to turn, so I asked for my mother's help.

My mother and father eventually got their licence for a pub. It was a run-down pub, in a run-down area. My mother hated it. But she signed a two-year contract. She was stuck there and had to see it through.

'Mum,' I said, holding Shelley in my arms, 'I haven't got anywhere to go. The landlady is selling up and has asked us to leave.'

My mother could see how desperate I was and said, 'I'll talk to your father.'

My mother didn't need to ask anyone what to do, she was the boss. It was Rosy she wanted to consult with. She didn't want to upset her. They depended on her for all the business work to be done; they had no idea how to do the tax and accounts for the pub.

Rosy was always out. She never helped out in the bar. She was above being a barmaid. My mother spoke to my father and said, 'They've got to go somewhere, Ed. We can't see them in the streets with a baby. Shall we let them move into Thorpedale Road?'

My father wasn't bothered; he didn't want to go back to the old life he had in the past. He was enjoying the pub life. He said, 'Might as well, mate. I can't see us moving back.'

Rosy had invested in a house of her own, so she didn't care.

The only one who had an opinion was my brother Billy. He said it wasn't fair. He and his wife would have liked the opportunity to have it, even though they were buying their own house. They were finding it hard to pay their mortgage and they also had a baby the same age as Shelley. They held a bit of resentment towards me, but they didn't want me to be without a home. We moved in straight away.

The place was in a right mess; it needed a lot of work doing. There wasn't any hot water system. The house was cold and damp; everything needed doing, and the rooms had old wallpaper.

It was a real challenge to get everything in a good living order. Having a baby and being pregnant made it hard for me. But we were grateful to have some where to live.

Robert lost interest in working on it. He had spent all his time and energy in our other flat. I did my best to clean the house up. I painted and decorated, but there were so many things that were in need of repair.

Robert was never at home any more; he lost interest in doing anything around the house and he kept me short of money. It got so bad that I had to pawn my engagement ring to get some material to make a maternity dress.

I asked him one day, 'Why do you go to work all dressed up?'

He made up some cock and bull story about meetings he took the minutes for; he said he had to look smart.

I was always on my own with Shelley, while Robert was out all the time. My friend Janet said, 'Katie, do you think he's having an affair?'

I couldn't for one minute contemplate that Robert could do such a thing. I said, 'No way; he loves me and Shelley too much.' I wouldn't hear of it.

Two weeks before the baby was due, I looked in Robert's pocket for some money to buy some food. I found a letter that changed my life.

It was from a girl named Linda. It read, 'I can understand why you wanted to leave me because of Shelley, but her, I hopes she chokes with her asthma.' My eyes started filling up with tears, but I read on. 'I'll swing for her if I ever see her.'

I broke down and was in shock. I felt like my blood had drained from my body. I couldn't think straight. I read on: 'I love you, Rob, and the last six months have been the best time of my life.'

Just to think that this person, whom I'd never met, was writing these things about me! Then the penny dropped: the nights out and going to work all dressed up, and when he was home, he couldn't look me in the face. He stayed in bed, and when he wasn't in bed, he put his face in a book.

I didn't know what to do. Here I was, expecting any time, and Shelley not two yet.

I put Shelley in her pushchair and went to my mother's. When my mother saw me, I looked a wreck. Her heart went out to me. 'What's the matter, Katie?' she asked.

I broke down on her shoulder and gave her the letter to read.

'Oh, dear, Kate! What you gonna do?'

'Divorce him, Mum.'

I left Shelley with her and went to the Citizens' Advice Bureau. I was like a headless chicken, going around Islington looking for solicitors that the bureau sent me to.

That night, I calmed down and the hurt turned into anger, but my heart was shattered.

When Robert came home from work, I said, 'Rob, sit down.'

He said, 'What's the matter?' He could see something was wrong and sat down on the sofa.

I calmly showed him the letter. He was taken back when he realised he was found out.

'What do you want me to do?' he said.

'Move out now!' I said in a cold voice. Robert tried to explain how it all came about and how sorry he was. He said, 'I wasn't looking for anyone else. I didn't mean it to go this far, but Linda kept following me around. She put her phone number on my car windscreen with her lipstick. I'm so sorry, Katie. I don't want to go. I love you and Shelley.'

I saw red, especially, when he mentioned 'her' name. He came over to me and knelt down. He had tears in his eyes and said, 'Please forgive me.'

He was so convincing, and I wasn't in a good position at that moment to be brave enough to kick him out. I was about to have a baby I didn't want to be on my own, bringing up two children. I calmed down and looked into his eyes to see if he meant what he said. I felt so much pain in my heart, just to think that he had been making love to someone else.

Then I said, 'Will you promise me not to see her again?'

Robert was very relieved to be forgiven so easily, but it wasn't as easy as he thought. At that time I didn't really have a choice.

I was not only carrying a baby now; I was carrying a broken heart. The pain went so deep. It joined the hurt that was already unresolved from my childhood. I was in a right mess. I couldn't forgive Robert. I just went along with having the baby, a day at a time.

~17~

My mother gave me a room in the pub to use while Robert was working because she was concerned about me being alone when the baby came.

At last my waters broke and I went into labour. I was ten days overdue.

Rosy had a car; she took me with my mother to the hospital. She felt sorry for me when she heard the news about the other woman in Robert's life and, believe it or not, she became supportive towards me. She wasn't all bad after all; when the chips were down she stood by her sister.

A nurse in reception greeted me. 'Where's your husband?' she asked.

No one knew how to get in touch with Robert when he was working. I was on my own. My mother and Rosy left me looking very sad and full of fear; I remembered how bad it was when I brought Shelley in the world. I walked down the corridor with the nurse holding my small case and my usual companion – fear.

Billy and Pam were looking after Shelley.

Childbirth in the 1960s wasn't an experience to be recommended. There were only two young midwives with me. I needed help to bring this baby into the world because there were complications. I tore as the baby was being born and passed out with the pain.

'Wake up, Mrs Barlow!'

I felt the midwife tapping my face and heard her say, 'Wake up and push, your baby is nearly here. We need you to give us one more big push.'

I'd been in labour for ten hours and was quite exhausted, and the gas and air weren't much help. I managed to push out my baby with all the strength I could muster.

It's strange how nobody talks about what a nightmare childbirth is. I guess it's a matter of pride.

It was another girl. We named her Daisy May.

Robert didn't turn up until the next day. He was disappointed because he wanted a boy. I was in a bad way after the birth of Daisy May; I went down into surgery to have an operation. I needed inner stitching.

Robert came in with some flowers and a new wedding ring as a symbol for a new beginning. But it wasn't long before Linda was on the scene again.

Robert hardly came to the hospital during those three weeks to visit me and his newborn daughter.

I was the only woman in my ward who didn't have her husband visiting and gloating over their newborn child.

I watched the fathers with their babies making a fuss of their wives, bringing them flowers and balloons and cards from well-wishers.

My baby was gorgeous, she slept and fed with no problems. But I, on the other hand, was in need of another operation, so I couldn't go home. The doctors told Robert that if I didn't have this operation, I wouldn't be able to have any more children.

I was very ill after Daisy's birth and wasn't able to show any feelings towards my newborn baby for the first two weeks.

I missed Shelley so much; I lost my appetite and was grieving for her. I wanted to go home.

Three weeks passed, and they felt like three months. Then the doctors discharged me.

Waiting for Robert to collect me seemed to last forever. I was dressed and waiting from 10 a.m. until 3 p.m. Finally he walked in without any thought of how long I was waiting.

'Where have you been?' I said, with a feeling of hopelessness in my heart.

'Asleep,' he answered.

That was when I thought, Words are cheap. Love is, as love does. I wasn't going to feel sorry for myself; I had two children depending on me now.

This was the beginning of the end of my marriage. I knew I was on my own now; I had the responsibility of my two daughters. No matter what Robert did from then on, I wouldn't be able to forgive him. I was biding my time.

When I saw a clip in my bed that wasn't mine, it was then that I made my mind up to leave him when I was ready.

Robert was still seeing his Linda and lying to me, making out his was at work. The rows and fights became frequent.

He wasn't interested in Daisy. He'd just walk past her little crib. She was so beautiful, I adored her, and I felt that I had to love her for the two of us. I knew what it was like to be rejected. The sadness I felt when I knew I'd lost Robert was unbearable. I hurt mostly for my babies because they too had lost their father.

Robert left home two weeks after I came home from the hospital. Even though I knew it would happen, it still hurt. My strength was failing me. I went to my mother's for support.

Rosy wasn't very happy, when she saw me turn up with my two children. She showed how she felt.

'I'm leaving if she moves in!' she shouted to my mother, making sure I overheard.

'I'll go home, Mum,' I said.

'No, you won't! Don't take any notice of her, she doesn't mean it.'

I was so relieved when I heard my mother say that. At last, I thought, someone is on my side…

My mother felt sorry for me and wanted to help me because of the children. My father, on the other hand, still looked up to Rosy and colluded with her. As far as he was concerned, she could do no wrong.

Rosy stayed away for three days just to prove her point. I went back home when she came back. I couldn't stay around with her performing all the time.

A few days passed, and I'd just got the children bathed and fed and was about to put them to bed when the doorbell rang. It was Robert. He said, 'Can I come in?'

I let him in because I wanted to talk about finances. Robert had more on his mind than money. He wanted to come back home.

I was like a ship without a rudder, not knowing where I was going at that time. I wasn't ready to be brave enough to throw him out. I had on my mind a big problem: how was I going to live alone without any money?

My children were my main concern. I had to do what was best for them, so I made some coffee and sat down to listen to what Robert had to say.

'I know I've hurt you, Katie, and don't deserve you, but I do love you and want to be with you and my children.'

All I heard was the last bit – 'be with my children'. I said, 'What if you go back with her again? I can't trust you any more. Please leave, Rob!'

He knew me far better than I realised. He said, 'I promise you I will never see her again.'

I thought, I don't have a choice at the moment. My children need their father and I'm broke.

I took him back, believing it was for the children. But I also needed the financial support from him. I didn't know how I could earn money with two small children to look after.

I let him back on the grounds that he never saw Linda again. It wasn't that easy.

The girl, Linda – who, by the way, was six years younger than me – wasn't going to let him go that easily.

The phone rang.

'Hello,' I said.

A girl's voice answered and said, 'Can I speak to Rob?'

I slammed the phone down. I was furious at the audacity of her phoning my home.

When Robert came home that night I was extremely angry. We had a big row, and he confessed that he'd been seeing her again. I threw him out again and this time I lost my temper and threw everything at him: cups, plates and a vase. Robert left again and went back to his lover.

Things went from bad to worse. My life became unmanageable. He came back and left many times before I finally refused to let him in again.

The poor children went through hell experiencing so much violence around them. The last straw was when Robert knocked me out cold at Daisy's christening.

The day started out well, with all the family and friends at the church. I looked a picture, dressed in a black lace dress with a large hat.

Everyone went back to the pub for the reception. My mother made some finger food, and as it was held in a pub there were plenty of beverages.

Robert was in one of his moods. He'd been drinking. He got angry with me because some man in the pub gave me a second glance.

'Get home *now!*' he said.

I went upstairs in the pub and refused to go. He followed me up and hit me so hard across the face that I went unconscious. The next thing I knew, I was over his shoulder being carried down the stairs.

I then knew it was time to get my life together and get this man out of it – if not for me, at least for the sake of my children.

I filed for a divorce on the grounds of cruelty.

I stayed at the pub, working as a barmaid and helping out in the home as much as I could to earn my keep. Having a baby and a two-year-old wasn't easy.

One night, after a hard day, I was fast asleep. Rosy came barging in the bedroom door, waking me up and shouting, 'You'd better get over to your place! Rob has a party going on, the house is full of people, and he'll wreck the place.'

I didn't know what to do. It was as if I was a robot doing what I was told and not thinking straight. 'How do you know?' I said.

'I drove past. Quick, I'll take you.'

I got myself dressed. It was about one in the morning. Rosy took me in her car and said, 'Go on – throw them out! It's your house, not his!'

I went inside and saw Robert, who seemed delighted to see me. But when I said, 'Tell all these people to leave, or I'll call the police! You have no right to do this!' he swore so much at me that I thought, What am I doing here?

I turned to go down the stairs and said to the people in my living room, *'Get out – all of you!'*

Then Robert hit me so hard around the head that he perforated my eardrum.

Rosy wasn't thinking straight when she took me to the house that night. Anyone with any sense would have known that he would attack me. He wasn't the man I married. He was an angry, violent man who couldn't control his temper, especially when he'd been drinking.

I was badly injured and couldn't hear properly for three weeks.

Robert left the house after that night and never returned.

~18~

It was Christmas Eve, 1963; I was working in the bar while the children were asleep upstairs.

It was a very, very busy night; the people were falling over themselves to get served. Billy, my father, my mother and I worked till we dropped.

The next morning I was in the kitchen just getting the children ready to visit their grandmother, who only lived a short distance from the pub, when Rosy came in.

She had a right mood on her. I'd worked really hard the night before in the bar. I thought she would have been appreciative for my helping, and it was Christmas Day – you know, 'goodwill to all men'. I didn't expect what happened next, but she verbally attacked me, saying, 'You're not wanted here; nobody has the courage to tell you, so I am.'

I looked at my father, who was standing next to her, waiting for him to say something in my defence. He turned away. That moment, I felt the pain of rejection from him that stayed in my memory for the rest of my life.

I thought, It's Christmas morning and I worked so hard in the bar last night. I had to crawl up the stairs on all fours to get to my bed. What's it all about? Why do Rosy and my father hate me so much?

I gathered my children and all my belongings and decided to go home. As I was leaving, my mother came up from downstairs and wanted to know what was going on. When she heard what had happened, she was furious and said, 'If she leaves, so will I!'

I felt a little better when I heard my mother say that. She was concerned for the children.

'I'll show them, Mum!' I said.

My mother saw the strength and determination in me. It reminded her of herself when she was on her own during the war. She said, 'That's right, girl, you show them!'

'I'll bring up my children on my own! I don't need those two – I don't need anyone.'

I got my things together and my two children, put them in the double pushchair and set off home in the freezing snow.

The house had been empty for some time and the water was frozen. It was like walking into a freezer. I took Daisy upstairs to her bedroom and placed her in her cot. Then I broke down and collapsed on my knees. I never in my whole life felt so down. I cried and vowed to myself, I will get my life together and make a home for my children; they will be the best dressed children in the street. I don't need anyone. I have my babies and I will make them happy if it's the last thing I do. No one will hurt me again.

I pulled myself together and lit a fire.

There was an oil heater that had paraffin in the back. It was a good way to get warm but the fumes were awful.

I wasn't alone. I felt God speak to me; it wasn't a voice from above, it was an inner voice – my voice – but it must have come from God because it was supportive, saying, 'Don't worry, Kate! I'm with you – everything will be all right.'

With every day that passed, I became stronger and wiser. I had no money from Robert, so I went to the social services. This was the most humiliating thing that I'd ever done. I felt so much shame, queuing for hours with all the down-and-outs. To make matters worse, the person behind the screen who decided if you were eligible for money said to me, 'What are you doing here? You don't look the type to be claiming.'

I was already feeling shame, and that statement only made me feel worse. I thought just like Scarlett O'Hara in the movie *Gone with the Wind*. ('I'll beg, steal or borrow; I'll never go hungry again.')

In 1964, the day came to go to court for my divorce. Robert came around the day before.

I wouldn't let him in. He stood on the doorstep for hours. I knew if I opened the door, it would start all over again, just like a merry-go-round.

I was well dressed in my tailored suit. I travelled by bus to the Strand. Not only was I there to get a divorce, but to get custody of my two children.

I met my solicitor at the courtroom. He introduced me to the barrister. 'This is Mrs Kathleen Barlow,' he said, and then, 'This is your barrister, Roger Harris. He just wants to go over a few things with you.'

We shook hands. 'Good morning,' the barrister said. 'The courtroom has been changed to the High Court, but don't worry, it's all a routine procedure. Just answer the questions when I ask you, Mrs Barlow, OK?'

He was a very nice man; he looked deep in my eyes when he spoke to me to see how I was feeling. I was feeling very strong. I had to get myself together for the sake of my children.

I looked around, wondering if Robert would come to claim visiting rights. He never showed. He probably didn't want to be cornered into paying maintenance.

My name was called. I nervously got up and went into the courtroom and sat down in a pew watching the case before me.

Then it was my turn; I was led to the witness box and was asked to repeat after the person carrying the Bible in his hand. He said, 'Repeat after me…'

I took off my brown leather glove, and held the Bible then said, 'I, Kathleen Barlow, swear to tell the truth, the whole truth and nothing but the truth, so help me God.'

The courtroom had the feel of authority, a strange atmosphere.

To think, there had been people tried for murder in this courtroom and had been sentenced to life in prison. All I'm here for is a divorce, I told myself. After that thought, my fear disappeared.

The barrister went through the statements and asked a few questions. Then the judge looked at me over the top of his specs and asked, 'Do you think that you can take care of your children all by yourself?'

I straightened my back, lifted my head high and replied, 'Yes, I do, My Lord.'

I was told to address the judge as 'My Lord' and not 'Your Highness', as some people did. The judge smiled and wrote something down.

It was all over, he granted the divorce and gave me full

custody of my children. I caught a taxi home and was proud of myself for my courage.

'It's over, Mum, I'm divorced now,' I said as I picked up Daisy. 'Where's Shelley?'

'She's playing in the front room with her doll's pram. How did it go, then?' my mother asked.

'Good. The judge asked me if I could look after the children on my own. The barrister said, "Normally judges don't say anything, they only make decisions." He gave me a lovely smile.'

I was getting onto my feet now; the only thing I needed was a sewing machine.

There was an old hand-operated Singer sewing machine at home, but it didn't have a base to sit on.

Then, one day when I was queuing outside the greengrocer's, I saw a tomato box, and thought, I wonder if that box will fit the old Singer sewing machine if I turn it upside down.

'Ron,' I said, pointing to the half-empty tomato box. 'Do you want this box?'

Ron, the greengrocer, had got to know me well by now and said, 'No. Why, do yer want it?'

'Yeah, I could use it for a project I'm working on.'

' 'Course yer can, take it. I'll take those toms out for yer.'

Home I went with my tomato box, and luckily the sewing machine fitted on it.

I bought a little electric motor for £2.

'Mum,' said Shelley, who was 2½ now, 'will you make me a skirt?'

I had some bits of material hanging around, so I said, 'OK, come here so I can measure yer.'

The skirt I made Shelley was cut in a full circle, so when she did a twist it flared out – just to her liking.

'Mum, can I have a pink one?' Shelley said.

'Sure, and a blue one if you like.'

I made baby clothes for Daisy, and also made some and sold them in the pub.

The children's clothes I made were as good as the designers'. All I had to do was look at a garment that was on display in a window. Then I'd copy it to perfection. I would have been a designer in children's wear if I'd been given the chance.

Money was scarce, so I bought remnants of material that were on sale outside the haberdashery shop.

My talent at designing was surprisingly good. I made everything I wore. Just as I'd promised myself, my children were the best dressed in our street; so was I. Even the dog had a matching coat from the bits of material left over from the trouser suits I made!

That Christmas, 1965, I was able to buy my children proper Christmas presents: a bike for Daisy and a doll's pram for Shelley.

'Mum,' Shelley said.

'Yes, Shelley,' I answered.

'Will I be able to see my daddy this Christmas?'

I remembered the time when I longed to see my daddy when I was five, so I knew how Shelley felt.

'I'm sure you will, darling. He'll be at Nanny Barlow's, you'll see.'

Robert saw the girls from time to time. Sometimes he'd be at his mother's house when they stayed with her on a Sunday morning. She looked after them while I worked in the pub.

Although Robert never paid me any maintenance money, I allowed him to see the children, simply because he was their father. I wanted them to have a relationship with him. However, his visits became less and less frequent. I really didn't know if he would be there at Christmas; I only hoped he would for their sake.

Shelley and Daisy missed having a father in their life. It was hard at school when other children spoke of their daddies and the things they did together. I gave my children all the love I could, but I couldn't be their father.

Working at the pub at weekends for £2 a session and doing a little homework on my sewing machine – the one on the tomato box – I was now earning enough to get by. All I wanted in life was to make my children happy.

One of our fondest memories were walking down Thorpedale Road one Christmas Eve, all three of us singing carols, out loud. We were singing 'While shepherds watched their flocks by night' and 'Away in a manger'. The kids liked 'Twinkle, twinkle, little star'. When I was happy, they were happy. This was a Christmas that I was able to hold my head high and enjoy the seasonal celebrations.

Shelley went to the nursery nearby, now that she was 3½. Daisy stayed at home with me. I got a cleaning job at Shelley's nursery in the evenings to earn extra cash.

Then Shelley became sick; she was having coughing spasms, and when she breathed in there was a crowing sound. She had whooping cough. Within no time Daisy caught it.

'Mum,' I said, 'I think Shelley has whooping cough.'

'Oh, Katie, no, that's bad. Call the doctor.'

We were really worried, and my mother couldn't get away to help.

The doctor examined my babies. He didn't say much, only, 'Keep them warm and give them plenty to drink, I have given them something to help them and I will call in tomorrow.'

I nursed my two children day and night for six weeks through this life-threatening disease. I was exhausted, and I had little help from my family. My father dropped some food off from time to time.

I was on my own. Even Robert didn't come to see his daughters. They could have died. The doctor came every day. I nursed my children back to health with prayer and all the loving tender care that I could summon up.

The inner voice was there every day encouraging me. 'It's going to be all right.' Whenever I heard that voice say, 'It's going to be all right,' I knew that it would be.

Robert married his lover, Linda, and had a child: a girl. He wanted a boy so much. It turned out that they couldn't have any more children because their blood didn't match.

The penny dropped later why Robert didn't come to see his children when they were sick. He was afraid he would pass on the disease to his baby.

The following year, I got my life back on track.

I was dressmaking during the day and doing bar work at weekends. I was earning enough money to buy an industrial sewing machine.

Then, gradually, I saved for a bedroom suite, a TV, a washing machine, a record player, and many more articles to make a comfortable home.

The only thing that troubled me was Shelley. She was asthmatic; she couldn't walk very far because of her short breath.

My asthma, thank God, left me when I left Robert. But Shelley, she suffered with asthma from the age of two. I attended the hospital every week, as she was under the specialist.

Shelley wasn't able to run around like other children. Her asthma was something she learned to live with all her life.

The universe was answering my prayer. My strength was most definitely growing, day by day.

The night-time was the worst time for me. My fear was my greatest enemy. It would just come and overwhelm me from out of the blue. My loneliness was one thing, but the fear I had when I was alone was soul-destroying.

Sometimes I'd bring it on myself by watching the TV late at night. The programme that was the most frightening was *One Step Beyond*. It was a late night show. When it ended I climbed up the stairs to bed with fear in me that almost paralysed me.

In the end I decided not to watch it and went to bed early with the children, who were in bed by eight every night.

They loved it, all sleeping in the same bed. I worked so hard to pay the bills and give my children all they needed to make them happy, so going to bed early was good for me.

Bath night was Friday. I still had the same old tin bath that my mother bathed me in. The bath was still hanging outside on the wall in the garden, and I would heat the water on the cooker in the same old metal buckets.

All I wanted was to be at home with my two children. I was wise enough to know that there wasn't anyone out there who would love my children as much as a real father would, so I made a decision that I'd put my life on hold until my children grew up.

In 1966, England beat West Germany 4–2 to win the world soccer cup. That was a day to remember; the whole nation celebrated. It was such a lively pub that weekend.

Mary Quant brought out miniskirts. I looked good in my miniskirt and my hair done up like a beehive. I was only seven stone four and looked much younger than twenty-six.

There were times when I gazed out of my living-room window and thought, There's a world out there that I've hardly seen. How I longed to be out meeting people! I was so lonely. I sighed and thought, One day I'll be free to come and go as I please, but not now. My life is around my children and I accept that for today, my responsibility is living to make them happy. God heard that prayer.

Shortly after my daydreaming, I had a desire to do something different. So it wasn't by chance I stopped outside a British School of Motoring shop and looked in the window to read the sign, 'Driving lessons £1 per lesson'. I found myself going inside. All I had on me was £3. The very next thing you know, I'd signed up for twelve lessons.

As you could guess, driving for the first time was quite funny. I didn't have any knowledge whatsoever about driving. We were too poor to own a car when I was young.

The instructor said, 'Don't worry, I have the controls as well as you, so just drive.'

I couldn't even steer. I said, 'I can't do this! I'm too scared to go into the road with all those cars going fast!'

'Go on, you can do it,' he said.

He held the steering wheel while I drove down the main road.

Slowly I got the hang of it, and before you knew it, I was driving!

Ten weeks later, I saved £50 and got myself a second-hand Morris Minor car. I paid a pound a week for the insurance for twenty-eight weeks.

There I was, driving around here, there and everywhere, which was great for Shelley, because of her asthma. I took her to school and went back and forth to the pub in comfort. Before that, I wore out my coat pushing the double pushchair back and forth. Now I could go around in style.

Having a car opened a new world for me and my two children. The three of us travelled about, watching out for the police, because I only had a provisional licence.

Children's car seats and safety belts weren't invented then, so Shelley and Daisy stood behind me when I was driving, helping me out by saying, 'Watch out, Mum, there's a police car!'

They did this until I got my full driving licence.

~19~

1968 was the year the Rev. Dr Martin Luther King Jr was assassinated. He was the US civil rights leader, and is remembered for his peace speech – 'I have a dream' – given to a crowd of over 200,000 at a civil rights march. The march was for organising the blacks' voting rights. The President, Lyndon Johnson, signed the Civil Rights Act, which was passed in August 1964, and another was passed in 1968.

This was also the year when Bobby Kennedy was shot. His brother, John F Kennedy, was shot in the head in 1963, the year Daisy was born. I had to ask myself, Why do people go around shooting each other? What kind of world do we live in?

My spiritual side would like to do something to make this a better world. The amount of people getting divorced and families spitting up was a major problem, not only for me but also for the world. If only I could make a difference, I thought.

I was twenty-eight when I met Andy. He was one of life's clowns, a tall, skinny bloke who wore black framed glasses (like Buddy Holly). He had the most wonderful personality. He made jokes and played stunts on people just to make them laugh.

I met him at a friend's house. I was feeling a little bored and thought I'd take the children for a drive. I went to see one of Rose's friends, Barbara. I rang the doorbell.

'Who's that?' a voice called from the top window of a three-storey house.

I stepped back and said, 'Hi, Barbara! It's me, Kate.'

'Hold on, I'll throw down the key,' said Barbara. 'Come up, Kate. It's lovely to see you.'

I went in and climbed the stairs but I accidentally opened the wrong door. Andy was with his friend, mucking about and trying on Barbara's dress.

He looked at me with a surprised expression on his face. I thought, He's a bit queer. I closed the door and said, 'Sorry.'

I forgot all about him and had a cup of tea with Barbara.

'How's life?' she said. 'The kids are getting big, how old are they now?'

'Shelley's six and Daisy's four.'

'Want some juice, girls?' The girls were very well behaved and politely said, 'Yes, please.'

'You coming to my party next Saturday, Kate?'

'I dunno,' I said. Just then the doorbell went.

Barbara went to the window and said, 'Hiya, Kat, come up!' Then she threw down the key again. Kat was a blonde girl, a typical cockney.

'This is Kate, Rosy's sister,' said Barbara. Everyone knew Rose; she was someone they respected because of her success in the nightclub.

Rosy had opened a club with the help of her boss. It became quite successful. The only problem was, it attracted all the so-called villains such as the Kray twins. When I was identified as Rose's sister, I got respected.

'Hello, nice to meet you.' Kat became quite friendly, but she had a motive.

She lived in the East End of London and it took her hours to get to Barbara's house. What with the party coming up, Kat had her sights on one of the guys who was going. As soon as she heard that I lived nearby and on my own, I became the target for her to stay with.

I fell for it after Kat showed some attention to Shelley and Daisy. Then she asked, 'I wonder if I could stay at yours next weekend, 'cos I'm going to Babs' party and I need somewhere to stay, as I live miles away.' I thought, She seems a good sort, I don't mind, and I could do with a bit of company. So I said, 'Sure, I'll give you my address.'

Kat wrote down my address and phone number, and said, 'See you next Saturday, then, in the afternoon some time.'

'OK,' I said. 'I'm off now, Barbara. I might come to the party – depends if I can get a babysitter.'

'Be sure you do! You could do with some fun, you never go out,' Barbara replied.

As I was leaving, this bloke who'd been cross-dressing in the other room was leaving the same time.

He followed me down the stairs and said, 'Hello, I hope you don't get the wrong idea about me. I'm not queer, I was just playing about with my mate. Are you Rose's sister?'

'Yes,' I said with a grin on my face, thinking about how I'd caught him out.

'I'm Andy, Nick's mate.' Nick was Barbara's brother.

'Hello, nice to meet you. I'm Kate and these are my two children, Shelley and Daisy.'

He smiled and said, 'Is that your car?'

I was proud to say, 'Yes.'

Then he got into a brand new Vauxhall. It was very impressive. It made my car look like an old banger, which it was.

The next day was Sunday, and I did the usual routine: took the kids to their grandmother's, and then went to work in the pub for the lunchtime trade.

I had dinner with my parents, and Shelley and Daisy ate at their grandma's. After dinner, I picked up the kids and went home.

I wasn't home long before the doorbell rang. It was Andy.

'Hello, can I come in?' he said. I was surprised to see him standing there in my doorway. I didn't have many visitors, so I was happy to see him. I smiled and said, 'Sure, come in. Do you want a cup of tea or coffee?'

'Thanks, I'll have some coffee, please – one sugar.'

He sat on the floor in the living room, kicked off his shoes and started to tell funny jokes. By the time he went home, I'd had laughed so much, my stomach ached. I had never laughed so much in my life before! Andy was like a breath of fresh air.

He came round the next day and entertained the children, then the next. By the time the end of the week came, Shelley and Daisy said, 'Mum, is Andy coming tonight?'

He obviously was interested in me, and did a smart thing by winning my children's affection first. He could see that if he wanted to get my attention, it would be through my children.

Kat turned up Saturday about four in the afternoon. She made herself at home and chatted away as if she had known me for years. She went on about some bloke she fancied; she was getting herself all geared up to see him at Barbara's party that night. She bought a new dress and dolled herself up just for him.

'What's his name?' I said.

'Andy.' Oh, I thought, not the Andy who's been on my doorstep all week... What shall I do now? She obviously liked him.

Andy had already planned on picking me up for the party. I didn't know that Kat was after him. I really didn't want to know him anyway, so I thought, I'll give him the cold shoulder.

He was on time, and when Kat saw him, she thought he was there for her.

Every time Andy sat next to me, I moved away. Poor Kat! She could see he fancied me and was quite put out.

When it was time to go, Andy and his younger brother, Pete, both made a fuss of me and took me home in their big posh car. Kat pushed herself into the car with me, saying, 'Wait for me!'

So she came too. Her plans of sleeping with Andy at Barbara's went right out the window.

She went home the next day, feeling cheated out of her opportunity to get Andy.

Kat became a regular visitor at the weekends, always hoping to see Andy. She had a big crush on him and was hoping to get his interest. But Andy was only interested in me.

He was eight years younger than I was. I didn't see him as a potential boyfriend. At first, I enjoyed his company as a friend.

He played with the children and made them laugh, which was a tonic for them. He brought laughter into my life, and his younger brother, Pete, was just as funny. The pair of them were a couple of comedians.

They were a bit of an embarrassment at times; like the time I was in a lift with them and they spoke to each other out loud, talking about things you wouldn't normally talk about, just to see people's reaction. They brought a smile to everyone they met.

They'd race me as I was driving, but they did it driving backwards.

I was no longer lonely. Someone out there heard my heart that day when I was gazing out of my window feeling lonely and sad. Now I had a car and friends that came to see me every day.

Kat and I became friends. She was the salt of the earth kind of girl. Shelley and Daisy loved her visiting us.

She worked in a bridal gown shop. One day she brought the girls each a netted headdress. They wore them playing out in the streets, riding their bikes up and down with bridal head veils on. It was a sight for sore eyes! It warmed the cockles of my heart to see my girls happy.

Andy took us to the coast, the countryside and sometimes fishing.

He did things like tying a dead fish on the end of Shelley's fishing line while she wasn't looking. She was so excited when she thought she'd caught a fish.

He played with them, and at bedtime he carried them both, one in each arm, up to the bedroom, and did a silly dance to entertain them.

In a short time Andy became part of the family. The children loved him. But I was feeling a little disturbed about the way I was looking forward to seeing him. My feelings were getting involved, so were my children's. Is this right? I thought. He's only a boy, just twenty years old. What of his parents? They wouldn't like their son being involved with a ready-made family. What shall I do?

Andy was coming on to me at every opportunity he had. He fell for me in a big way and worked hard to get me to respond.

It was a strange affair, what with Kat coming over nearly every weekend just to see him. There he was, making advances to me behind Kat's back, and I made out his was only a friend. I didn't want to hurt her feelings.

I decided to tell Andy how I felt.

'Andy, I do think we should see what's going on here. I'm not sure if this relationship should go any further. I'm beginning to rely on you to come over, and I don't like that.' Then, I told him, 'It would be for the best if you didn't come over any more. Your parents won't approve of me. I'm eight years older, and have two children.'

Andy worked for his father in their family business. The new Vauxhall car was his father's. They manufactured shoes – shoes that were made for the NHS (National Health Service). They were surgical shoes for the people who had problems with their feet. Andy was very skilled at making these shoes. He worked hard.

He was very upset when I stopped him from coming back. He came the next evening and slept in his car outside the house all night. The next morning I was shocked to discover what he did.

'Andy, what the hell are you doing here?' I said.

'I don't care about what anyone says about us, I just want to be in your life,' he said.

I sighed. 'Well, OK, let's see what happens and take it one day at a time.'

How could I stop him? He was such a joy to be with, and Shelley and Daisy adored him. I was once again in a relationship – this time with a younger man – and had a ready-made family. There was bound to be trouble.

~20~

The relationship with Andy went from strength to strength.

I was right: his parents didn't approve at all.

On Sundays, Shelley and Daisy were at their Nanny Barlow's house.

After the lunchtime session, I was invited to Andy's home for dinner with his family.

His parents were quite well off, due to Andy's hard work over the past five years. The business was only successful because he worked all hours and got very little pay.

The deal was he was a 50% partner. He worked, and his father put in the cash. Andy worked on promises from his father, who was only out to use him.

He was promised a sports car, which never came. He was promised a rise, which never came.

'Hello,' Andy's mother said as she opened the door.

'Come in. I'm Audrey,' she said, with a northern accent. I smiled and went into the kitchen and met Jenny and Jackie, Andy's sisters.

'Hello,' said the younger sister with a smile. 'I'm Jenny.'

I looked much younger than my years and was well dressed.

Jackie came in and just smiled. She had all her belongings in a corner of the room. She was asked to leave and find a place of her own, so she wasn't in a good space at that time.

Jackie was a year older than Andy and just as tall. Her hair was back-combed to the point that it stood up to make her even taller.

Andy had another elder brother who was living in Liverpool with his wife. He was the black sheep of the family, because he got married instead of working in the family business.

Ken, Andy's father, was a tall man with a stern look on his face. He had been a sergeant major in the war. He wasn't very pleasant to me. He hardly spoke at all. I felt very uncomfortable around him. Audrey, on the other hand, was quite pleasant.

I sat down to dinner with Andy's family, all but Jackie. It was a strange set-up; I knew they didn't approve of me, but they didn't let it show. They didn't ask about my children once. In fact, they acted as if I didn't have any kids. I was unaware Andy wasn't ready to let the cat out of the bag yet.

One day, Andy's father approached me with a proposition. He gave me the upper part of a shoe and asked, 'Do you think you could make this?' He was having trouble getting someone to do the stitching work on the surgical shoes they made. The person they had working for them was an alcoholic and kept letting them down.

I was pleased that I was asked. I thought, How much will he pay me?

Ken's offer was more than I expected. The children were both at school now, so I could work part-time for him.

Now that I was earning a good living and had a man in my life, the table was turning for me.

Rosy thought she'd do a little stirring one day. She and my mother took it upon themselves to bring the children to the factory while I was working. They knew my children were not involved in Andy's family.

Encouraged by Rosy, my mother said, 'Go on and get Mummy – she's in there working with Andy.'

They came running in looking for their mum, calling, 'Mum! Andy!'

The look on Ken's and Audrey's faces when the kids came in was indescribable. Ken's mouth dropped. They knew now that I had children; the truth had hit home.

After that, Andy had a problem with his father. He wouldn't let him use the car; he didn't give him enough money because he said I was using him.

He tried to get Andy to break up with me using every angle he knew. Yet while all this was going on behind my back, he still wanted me to work for him. In time the storm calmed down and no more was said.

Two years passed. I said to Andy one day, 'Andy, you know I'm getting on for thirty now, and if you want to stay with me, don't you think that time is running out for a family of our own?'

I was also thinking about Andy. If he wanted to have children and stay with me, the biological clock was ticking for me.

Andy said, 'I have been thinking myself about getting married, but I'm afraid to upset my mother, she has a weak heart.' (So he was told. She was a bit of a fraud when she wanted attention.)

Andy thought hard about what he wanted and took some time out to see how he thought about getting married.

'Let's do it – let's get married, Kate. You get a marriage licence and let's go for it.'

I was well in love by then and Andy loved me. He was good to the children, so it felt right to get married and have a child of our own.

Well, when Andy told his father and mother he was going to marry me, all hell broke out! Andy was instructed time and time again not to marry me. Evan Pete, his brother, got on the bandwagon and tried to break us up.

Once again I got the old rejection demons in me again. I thought long and hard about getting married to Andy. In my heart I knew that I should have let go and moved on long ago, but we loved each other now, so it wasn't that easy. I thought I'd let Andy decide what the best thing was to do. The ball was in his court.

He became confused because of all the brainwashing from his family. He took more time out to think what he should do.

He loved me far too much to let me go now.

We were married in a register office in mid-November 1970. Shelley and Daisy stayed with my mother that day in their new house. The pub days were over for my parents; after six years they felt they needed a rest. The council wanted to pull down the pub to make a park area, so they gave them a council house in Hertfordshire.

I made my wedding outfit, a mini–maxi. That was the fashion in the seventies; the dress was a mini and the matching coat was maxi.

I chose a coral colour. I also made dresses for Shelley and Daisy in red velvet with white lace collars, decorated with a lace cravat dangling down the front.

There was only one person who turned up at the register office that day – Nick, Andy's mate.

Andy never wore suits; he was always in jeans. But this day he put himself out and bought a suit, off the peg, for £20. The sleeves were a little short, but that didn't matter. He was a happy man, and was determined to make a go of being a family man. I was the love of his life, even though it meant trouble ahead from his family.

There we were at the register office, all set to take our vows to each other, when we realised we didn't have any witnesses. So Andy stopped a couple of people on the street. Not many people would have had the audacity to go up to complete strangers and say, 'Excuse me, would you be our witness? We're getting married.'

'Sure, we'd love to,' the strangers said.

This time around I believed Andy was the right man for me. He had his faults, but after Robert's swearing, womanising and violence, Andy's crudeness was acceptable; after all, the jokes he told wouldn't be funny without being a little crude. He never stopped trying to make you laugh. Everyone who met him liked him.

Andy looked into my eyes after we were pronounced man and wife and said, 'I do love you, Kate.'

I answered, 'And I love you too, Andy.'

We had our wedding breakfast at the top of the GPO Tower to celebrate our special day.

Barbara had one of her parties that night so Andy, Nick and I celebrated that evening at Barbara's. Kat was there and wished us all the very best.

The morning after the wedding Andy looked into his pocket to see what cash he had left. All he had was a shilling! This is what we started our married life with: one shilling.

Andy went back to work on the Monday morning and came back home a few hours later. His father insulted my name by calling me a whore. Andy said, 'That's my wife you're talking about,' and walked out.

Neither of us had a job now, and I couldn't get family allowance because I was married. So money was short.

Rob visited the children the following week. I thought it was time for him to pay towards their keep. I told Andy what I was about to do. He said, 'Kate, don't worry about him. He won't want to give you anything now that you're married to me. I'll look after them from now on, let him go.'

I didn't want Robert to stop seeing his children, as it was important for Shelley and Daisy to have their father in their life. But it wasn't right that he didn't pay for their keep. I thought it was time he helped out financially. I wrote a letter to Robert asking him to go to the court if he wanted to see his children again. I didn't think for one minute that he would walk away and never come back. This was a shame; his daughters needed him now more than ever. I never saw Robert again.

Andy advertised in the local newspaper to do any odd jobs.

He even went to claim for benefit, but after seeing a long queue he left. He wasn't the type to claim.

The work he got from the ads helped a little. I did sewing again. Between us we managed to keep our heads above water.

Then one day, out of the blue, there was an unexpected caller. The doorbell rang. It was Mr Davis. Andy had done work for him when he was working with his father.

'Hello, Mr Davis. What are you doing here?' Andy said.

'I heard you left your father and were looking for work,' he said.

'Come in, please sit down.' The house was all topsy-turvy because we were decorating. I felt a bit embarrassed with all the mess. He didn't notice. He was there on a mission.

'Andy, I can get you work from the hospitals if you want,' said Mr Davis.

Andy was surprised to hear this, as Mr Davis was giving his work to his father. He said, 'That would be great, Mr Davis, but what about me dad? You're one of his contractors?'

'Look, son, I don't like to say this, but your father and I fell out. He put the pressure on me for a cheque when I hadn't got the money through from the Ministry of Health. He said if he didn't get the cheque by the end of the week, I could take my work elsewhere. To tell you the truth Andy, I can't get anyone to do the work as well as you. You'll be doing me a favour as well. Do you want the work?'

I didn't say anything, but was hoping Andy would take the

offer. We needed an opportunity to start up our own business, and besides that, I was two months pregnant.

Andy shook Mr Davis's hand and agreed to pick up some work as soon as possible. Then he thanked him very much for coming all the way from Surrey.

Andy told his brother, Pete.

'Yer'd better not let Dad find out you're doing work for him,' Pete said.

'What can I do, Pete? I need to earn some money.'

'Erm, I know; but look, Andy, you know what Dad's like. He's too proud to eat humble pie. What if I tell him that you said if he wants some help, you'll be happy to do some work for him at home?'

'That will be great, Pete; will you get my tools and some leather?'

Pete was the go-between for Andy and his father.

Ken, my father-in-law, was finding it hard not having Andy around to do the work. Pete wasn't a shoemaker like his brother. When Pete told Ken the offer Andy had made, he was only to please to cooperate.

I was now in the shoe-making business with Andy. We started making shoes at home. I was stitching the uppers while Andy made the shoes to order. He also did the bracing for his father's shoes.

The bedroom was used for the workshop. Andy made shelves for the leather on the landing. The cellar was used for lasts. When it came to the finishing, Andy went to the local shoe repairers and asked if he could use their machinery. Within six months we had our own shoe repairing shop. The rooms above the shop were used for the surgical shoe manufacturing.

When Ken heard about the work Andy was getting from Mr Davis, he stopped giving work to Andy and cut off all contact with him.

In September 1971, Melissa was born: a beautiful 7 lb 2 oz baby girl.

She was the sunshine of Andy's life. He adored her. She was a gorgeous baby with eyes so blue and lashes so long.

Shelley and Daisy were delighted to have a baby sister at last.

They had been wanting for me to have a baby for ages.

Andy came home every lunchtime just to see Missy. He played with her and boasted about her to all his friends. The only person he couldn't show her off to was his father. He missed his family very much. But Ken was adamant he still didn't want to know his son.

Andy and I sneaked Missy over to see Audrey while Ken was at work.

Audrey was so proud of her little granddaughter but was terrified of her husband finding out. She was a bit of a wimp, under her husband's thumb.

Six months went by and I dressed Missy up in her pettiest pink dress and went to Ken's factory with Andy, hoping he would want to see his granddaughter.

Andy took Missy to the doorway and said, 'Do you want to see your granddaughter, Dad?'

Ken pointed his finger at the door and shouted, 'Get out!' and Andy came way with tears in his eyes.

As time passed and the cash was rolling in, Andy started drinking. He celebrated his success every weekend with party after party. He had many friends and stayed out till late. His excuse was that he'd worked for his father all through his teenage years and was making up for his lost youth.

After a while, I began to feel uneasy about the amount of alcohol Andy was consuming. I stopped drinking myself because it was becoming too frequent. I was hoping Andy would slow down, but the more concern I showed, the more he became angry and the more he drank.

A year later, just before Missy's second birthday, Ken got Pete to have a word with Andy. He wanted to have a meeting with him. His business was going downhill fast and he wanted to sell up.

Also, Pete met a Canadian girl and wanted to get married and live in Canada. The only person who would be interested in this line of work was Andy.

They made a date to meet.

Pete, Andy and Ken got together for the first time in two years. The meeting was about the business. Andy agreed to buy his father out for £2,000. His father also wanted Andy to give him a job and to pay all his expenses on his car, including petrol; and one more thing – to give his mother twenty pounds a week. The reasoning behind the deal was that Ken had started up the business. He said Andy wouldn't be where he was if it wasn't for him. They did a gentlemen's handshake on the deal and agreed to Ken's terms.

Ken wrote a letter to me. It read:

Dear Kate

I was hoping that we could start again and put the past behind us. Audrey and I would like to invite you and Missy to dinner this Sunday.

Yours sincerely, Ken

There wasn't any invite for Shelley and Daisy, or any apology for the harm done to me and my children and for Missy missing out on her grandfather's affection for the first two years of her life. But still, it was a step forward for Andy to have his family back in his life again. So I accepted the dinner invitation. Shelley and Daisy stayed with their grandmother.

The family made a special Sunday lunch; it was the first time Ken had met his granddaughter. They all clubbed together to buy Missy a rocking horse for her birthday. She was two years old.

Everyone played happy families, but in my heart I knew they were only doing this to get out of the sinking ship they were in.

1973 marked the beginning of the worst time in Andy's life. The animosity that was held in Andy's parents' minds was pure evil. Instead of being happy for him about his success in business, they were jealous. The more we succeeded, the more it stuck in their throats. Money was their God.

At least twice a week, Andy came home from work completely stressed out over the pressure his father put on him. Whisky was Andy's way to deal with the pain of a lifetime of disappointment.

He spent his whole life trying to get his father to be proud of him and approve of him. All he wanted was his praise. I was in the middle of the fire of hatred, envy and jealousy. It became quite ugly.

Ken, being an ex-sergeant major in the army, didn't know how to love and care for his children. He raised them in a military style. He didn't know how to be compassionate and praise his sons; he saw that as a weakness. All he knew was to punish them if they stepped out of line.

Audrey manipulated her sons to get her own way. She used the threat of telling their father if they didn't do as she asked.

Underneath, Andy resented his mother for the way she treated him, and hated his father for the way he used him. Like me, he was starved from love and affection when he was growing up.

I heard it said that like has a way of attracting like – something like a mirror reflecting one's own injuries – in life. Andy's childhood reflected my childhood.

Maybe this is how the universe works, bringing the defect to the light for the purpose of healing. The poison has to be cleared before healing can take place.

Nature is a strange thing. The power of healing is a mystery to the world. The one thing we can depend on is that when we hurt our physical body, e.g. break a leg, we don't have to tell ourselves how to heal the break. The pain somehow sends a message to the brain, then immediately our body sets out to heal the injury; no one has to say, 'Oh, I've broken my leg – send the healing army to fix it!' It's a kind of miracle, the way the body works. So who knows what kind of mystical action goes on when the hurt in on the inside?

I didn't understand then about the whys and wherefores. All I knew at that time was everyone I loved turned against me.

~21~

In 1974 I had a son. We named him Matthew. He was born when Andy's drinking was beginning to take its toll. Andy's character was changing. The alcohol was having an effect on him, to the point that he was losing his sense of right and wrong.

He let Daisy drink too much wine when she went out with him to celebrate the birth of Matthew.

She phoned me up while I was in hospital and said, 'Mum, Dad's making me go to school and I feel sick.' She was sobbing her little heart out.

'Why do you feel sick, darling?' I said.

'I drank too much wine last night.'

I was furious. Once again, the winds of change were blowing in my life. I thought Andy would love me for ever. But no, it wasn't long before he was looking for something better. The demons were working on him through the alcohol he consumed.

It wasn't long before he made a pass at Sally, the young shop assistant. She was seventeen. Andy was twenty-seven. She was ten years younger; history was repeating itself again.

The nightmare that followed went on for years.

I was in the way, and Andy wasn't prepared to pay the price of a divorce. He wanted his house, his children, his business and his lover.

When I found out about Sally, once again my heart broke. I blamed the alcohol. I slowly watched this man change from being a loving joyful husband to an ugly, hateful man.

All Andy wanted to do was have parties and go out with his friends. He kept his lover for the afternoon shift.

I didn't know what to do. I didn't want to break up my family again. The damage that was done to Shelley and Daisy was undeniable – a lifetime of mental scarring. I didn't want Missy and Matt to go through the heartache of a broken family.

I searched everywhere for help. If I could have, I would have climbed the highest mountain to get help to save my marriage.

Nobody in the family wanted to know. They weren't there when Andy had his rages. They didn't see how his spoke to me and interrogated me about my past and called me names.

It was as if Andy wasn't there any more. Instead there was this stranger with hatred in his eyes and an evil expression on his face. No, it wasn't my beloved Andy, he was gone. I was up against something far beyond my understanding.

As time went on, my father became sick with cancer. He put up a fight for three years before this disease finally took him.

He passed away. My mother was on her own now. Rosy stepped in to take over the decision making for her. Then she decided to take her home to live with her.

By then Rosy was married with two children, but her marriage was on the rocks, so she was happy to have her mother there to help her bring up her children. I still felt the animosity between my sister and me.

It was different with my mother. She was always concerned for her grandchildren, and gave a kind word now and then to me, which was surely welcome.

Rosy was in the publishing business and was doing well, until her marriage came to an end.

It was drink related; she had the same problems as I had, watching her husband disappear under the affluence of alcohol.

A little while after they separated, Rosy started her own business. She took the responsibility of bringing up her children by herself, and at the same time look after my mother. The only way she coped was to work from home. She needed all the help she could find.

I, being in financial need, volunteered to work for her. I had to eat humble pie because Rosy was cold and controlling. She was a powerful businesswoman and had little time for my problems. It was my mother who was the peacemaker. Rosy loved her mother and wanted to keep her happy, so she tolerated me for two reasons: one, I was a hard worker; and two, Mum wanted to help me because she knew I was struggling financially.

I worked for my sister, and in time the gap that was between us gradually began to close. But it was hard for me to be the poor one while Rosy was making a pile of money and splashing it out on holidays abroad with her children and my mother, while I stayed home running the business and taking care of the dogs until they returned.

Andy and I were virtually separated. He was having the time of his life with his young mistress. He spent a fortune on the so-called 'good times', while I was given just enough to put the food on the table and put petrol in my car.

I used the little cash I earned from Rosy to help Shelley from time to time. She was working towards a degree and had rent to pay.

Then there was Daisy. She wanted to get married. I helped pay for her wedding by getting into debt. I made her wedding dress and six bridesmaids dresses and paid for their honeymoon.

Andy didn't want to know. He was against Daisy's boyfriend.

He was out for trouble the evening they got engaged. I saved up for a party for them and Andy ended up fighting the boy. I was in the room when it all started. Andy just picked on him and laid into him like a jealous lover.

There were many violent outbursts towards me that made me ill. I was emotionally, mentally and physically sick. But I still didn't leave.

Where could I go? I had no money or education, and nowhere to live. The only way I could get my needs met was to divorce Andy. Then, I would have my half of everything we had built up over the years. I didn't want to do that. I didn't want to destroy our home and family – or what was left of it. I hung on and I prayed and prayed for help.

I tried the church to see if I could call on some outside power to help me with my problems with Andy's drinking.

'Pray,' said the vicar.

'But I do pray!' I replied. 'I pray all the time for God's help, but nothing changes. My husband still drinks and treats me badly.'

I lost myself in the church for a few years in the hope that I could get God to help me.

Andy hated my Christian beliefs.

One day I took the children to church with me in the hope

that they would be protected from the rages and rows that were going on, only to find that when I got home all my clothes had been thrown out, and Shelley's and Daisy's beds had a bucket of water poured on them.

I went to the solicitors to file for a divorce because I felt I couldn't cope any more. The children were still underage, so I was entitled to stay in the house, which consisted of six bedrooms, two bathrooms and a swimming pool.

Being a third partner in the business, which was turning over quite a substantial amount of money, I should have easily had enough to live on. But although on paper I was financially independent, it was a different story in real life. I didn't get to see a penny of Andy's empire. All in all, I would have been much better off separated. Andy knew this. So he thought he'd better play his cards right.

'Kate, I think we need to talk,' he said one afternoon. My health wasn't too good under the circumstances; I wasn't eating much and I couldn't sleep. So Andy's timing was spot on.

'OK, Andy, I'm listening.'

'You know I don't want to split up our family,' he said.

'But I can't take your excessive drinking,' I said. 'You change when you drink.'

'What about your religion?' Andy replied.

'All I do is go to church and ask for help because of your behaviour.'

'I'll tell you what: if I stop drinking, will you stop going to church?' Andy said, looking so sincere. I was only going to church in the hope that God would intervene and help him stop. Now he was saying that he was about to stop drinking, so I was listening. I was thinking of the children once more.

'You say that now, but if I take you back, you might start again and I will lose my claim of "unreasonable behaviour" – which is the grounds for the divorce. How can I trust you?' I said. 'And what about Sally?'

'Kate, Sally doesn't mean anything to me. She's just a kid; nothing happened between us. I don't want to break up our family. Why don't we get some help from a counsellor?' Andy seemed sincere, just like his old self, for a while. So it was easy for me to believe in him.

My weakness was my children. I thought, If only I can have some kind of harmony in the house, it will be worth it for the children's sake. When they are older and don't need a mother to take care of them, I can think of what I will do with my life then. We had a lot to lose.

'OK, Andy, I will postpone the divorce and see how things go, but Sally will have to go.' Andy pulled me towards him and kissed me. Sally was sacked.

The strangest thing happened when Andy and I were having our sessions with the counsellor.

All the things that I wanted to talk about were turned around in such a way that it looked as if I was the perpetrator and Andy was the victim. The counselling was a waste of time. In no time Andy was drinking again.

1987, I heard of an organisation (Al-Anon) that supported the families of alcoholics. I thought I would give it a try.

The church wasn't the answer for me. No matter how much I prayed, I didn't find any way out of the pain and despair that was inside me. In fact there were many times I felt suicidal. I always held onto my beliefs, though. Ever since I was a child I'd believed in Jesus.

Deep down, I felt a love inside me that often spoke to me. I thought it was my voice encouraging me to keep going and not to give up.

'This will soon pass.' It must have been God talking to me, because it was clear, gentle, positive and simple. I could hear myself say, 'Be still and know that I am God.' I wasn't aware at that time just how close to God I was.

The meetings were full of women. They were for men too, but this meeting only had women there. About ten ladies sat around a table. One of them was the spokeswoman. She opened the meeting, and then each one of the other ladies read from a little book.

One of the women spoke about her experiences of living with someone addicted to alcohol. Following that, the others came in one at a time to share comments about their life and how they felt. At the end of the meeting I thought, They're speaking about me! That's how I feel! I identified with the drink problems that they had with their loved ones.

At last, I thought, I had found a place where I was understood. I now felt that I wasn't alone any more.

That night on my way home I felt as if a heavy load was lifted from my shoulders. I thought, At last I've found the right place to go. I do believe I belong here. These ladies were living with someone close to them who drank and they had a life. They seemed to be happy. I wanted some of what those ladies had: *a life!* I wanted my life back.

~22~

The years passed. I stuck with my marriage, just as I said I would. I couldn't have done it without the support of those meetings. I went twice a week in the hope that one day Andy would wake up to his drinking addiction.

I was getting emotionally stronger as the weeks went by, living for the day when I could be free from the neglect I was experiencing from Andy.

He was never home. If he wasn't in Canada with his brother and his family, he was in some other country with his girlfriend, Sally, hoodwinking me into believing he was having a break from the pressure of the business. How he managed to keep the business going, no one knows.

The more I tried to get Andy to see that he had a problem, the more he became angry. In the end I learned to detach – this being the changed attitude I learned from the ladies at the meetings.

But the strain on me was hard. I was determined to stay put until my children grew up. Missy and Matt were still at school.

Daisy was married now, and Shelley was still at college. She was very academic; her gift was in her artwork. She was working towards a degree in fine art.

Andy's lifestyle was totally self-centred, spending money on expensive clothes and jewellery. Meals out with his friends was one way of hiding his drinking problem.

The debts were growing. Financially, we were going down fast. The business was in so much debt, about £300,000 in all.

Then the crunch came. The bank manager told Andy he couldn't do any more business and told him to put the shop up for sale and sell his house to clear his debt.

Andy wasn't about to do that, so he made most of the staff redundant and worked himself. I stepped in and worked all hours. I learned how to cut keys.

The shop wasn't only a shoe repairers; we also fitted locks and cut keys.

I did the serving, cutting keys, booking in lock jobs and stitching the uppers for the surgical shoe manufacturers. I was fighting for my family's welfare. Andy's drinking and womanising put so much of a strain on the business that we were going downhill fast.

Meanwhile, Andy was doing a disappearing act with his lover; unbeknown to me, he was living a double life, leading Sally on to think that when the children were older he'd leave me and marry her.

At the end of two years my hard work paid off. We got the business up and running again.

I also worked hard to hold my family together.

I had learned by now that things weren't going to change. Andy's desire to drink was stronger than his mind. Even though his body was suffering with the alcoholic poisoning, the compulsion to drink was stronger. There wasn't anything I could do to stop my marriage from going downhill.

I was preparing myself to leave and thought that if Andy didn't stop drinking by the time Matt was eighteen, I would have to go.

The following years were very difficult; many times, I wanted to run away, but Andy would just pull me back with his promises. He knew it would cost him a lot if we got a divorced.

The children were just as unhappy as I was.

The fights and threats of divorce were hard to tolerate. I couldn't count the number of times young Matt was told his parents were getting a divorce. This affected his mind so much he became insecure and lost confidence in himself.

I was slowly breaking down. Andy was always looking for a reason to explode and I wasn't clever enough to see it coming.

It was as if there was a spiritual warfare going on. Somehow this disease knew when and where to come in and say and do the very thing that would cause an impact that cut deep. It was a mental sickness, because of the insane behaviour that went on.

The literature in the group meetings says, 'It's a progressive illness.' I felt deep down that I would have to do something soon, because I was spiritually dying.

One night I had a dream. I was in a foreign country, somewhere like Morocco. I was with Andy in a marketplace.

Then I wandered off, leaving Andy bargaining with some Arab. When I looked around for Andy I couldn't find him. I called out to him, but he was nowhere to be seen. I began to panic; I went up and down the market square calling him. I couldn't find him.

It began to get dark and the traders packed up and went home, leaving me in the dark. I was petrified and lost.

Then I had a vision that I saw Andy's hand in the dark reaching out to me, but I couldn't catch hold of it. Then it disappeared.

I woke up in a sweat with tears rolling down my cheeks. The dream was an omen of what was about to happen in my life.

My meetings were a lifeline to me. I respected the guidelines that helped me detach from the devastation that this mental disease caused. I learned to accept the things that I couldn't change.

There are so many families and relationships torn apart because of this 'mental disease'.

I also began to read self-recovery books that gave me hope.

At first I struggled to read, but the more I read the easier it became.

Living with a person who drank and had mind-changing behaviour made me confused.

I was desperate to find a way forward and get out before I went out of my mind.

The twelve-step programme was suggested to me. I was reminded that there are no halfway measures for it to work. You have to be ready for a life-changing experience.

I understood the steps, but wasn't ready to work them, because I knew that I had to be free from the disease for them to work for me. This meant leaving my husband.

I still remembered the man I'd loved and married, and wasn't ready to give up the hope that he would return if he stopped drinking.

All my visions and expectations of having a happy family life, which I always dreamed of, were hard to let go.

In 1991, Matt was coming up to eighteen. I was coming to the end of my tolerance with Andy. But what really made my mind up to leave was when Andy left me for five months to be with Sally.

My heart broke once again.

I sat at the kitchen table one day and thought back over the previous few years. Going in and out of this relationship was totally unreal; it was real madness.

I can't go on like this any longer, I thought. I must get help to leave. But every time I went to do something about it, Andy somehow stopped me. It was as if I was in some kind of bondage.

I prayed a different prayer this time. I said, 'God, I can't do this any more. Show me a way out so I can have a life without all this emotional pain. I can't do this alone. Please help me.' Then I thought, which could have been God talking to me again, *Send me a lover to help me leave. Because that will be the only way to put a stop to Andy's sweet-talking me into staying…*

Then I bunched my hand into a fist and slowly opened it. In my mind I was letting go of my marriage and all my connections to it.

I'd always been faithful to Andy. I believed in fidelity. I believed in God, and thought for as long as I stayed faithful to Andy there would be some hope that he would wake up to what was happening between us and snap out of it. But I was losing hope; Andy wasn't going to change. I'd come to the end of the road.

Matt was eighteen now. This was my deadline. Missy was engaged, and Matt was at college. Shelley had her own place and Daisy was married.

I worked it out that I should be financially secure when I got my third of the business and half of the house. On paper it looked good.

By the time the house was sold and I was bought out of my share of the business, after the mortgage was paid I would be better off living on my own.

But it didn't work out like that, no way. Andy was a clever man. He worked out how to get away with the house, the business and the building the business was in. Also, he got out of paying maintenance.

He went to a West End solicitor's. It cost him £25,000 to find a way to cheat me out of my entitlement. He was out to destroy me in every way he could.

He was hurt and angry about the way I abandoned him for another man. Not once did he think about how he'd abandoned me, year after year, and how he cheated on me and suppressed me, using me for his own gain. No, his mental disease wouldn't let him see his part in the deterioration of our marriage. I had no chance. I was no match for him, especially now that I had a lover.

Yes, God did send me a lover: Cliff.

I met him while Andy was on one of his geographic drinking trips. He was a Persian man much younger than me.

He was very understanding when I confided in him.

I poured my heart out to him, I told him how I felt and how I tried so many years to cope with Andy's mind-changing personality. I said, 'Cliff, I want to leave, but every time we agree to end the marriage, I'm pulled back in again. I need help to get free.'

'I will help you though this,' he told me.

He had soft brown eyes, with so much compassion and sincerity. I trusted him to stand by me while I challenged my husband to end our marriage in a fair and square way.

~23~

I asked my mother if I could stay in her house.

It had been empty for a number of years after my father's death. My mother was living with Rosy.

'Mum, can I stay in your house until I get my settlement through? Then I will have enough money to buy my own place.'

'Well, OK, just until you get sorted, Kate. I don't want you to make any changes to the place.'

I moved my things in, but made a big mistake by telling Rosy about Cliff, thinking she would understand how I needed his help at this moment.

Rosy was worried that I would stay in my mother's house and wouldn't be able to get me out. She wasn't about to believe that I would be in a position to buy it.

My mother made a will for her house to be sold and divided between her four children. If I stayed and had nowhere to live, they wouldn't be able to make me move. It would mean a court case to get me to leave. My mother knew if that was the case, my brothers wouldn't go to court to throw me out.

Rosy intervened and went with my mother to the house and threw out my things. I came back just in time to see my belongings being thrown in a black plastic bag in the hallway.

'Mum! What are you doing? I'm your daughter!' How can you do this to me?' I cried.

'Go back to your husband. I don't want you here,' she said.

I was so shocked by what had just happened. I had nowhere else to go. I thought, I'll go back home until I find my own place. But by then Andy knew about Cliff. He said, 'You can't do this, you can't come back. You must find a place of your own.'

I realised that I had to move on. Before I could think what my next move was, I thought, I'll take a bath, gather my thoughts then look for a flat.

But Andy was so angry he changed the locks to the house

while I was sorting out my belongings from my mother's house.

I didn't know what to do and where to go at that time, so I broke the window to get in. As it was my house, I didn't know I was breaking the law.

Meanwhile, Andy called the police and told them a bunch of lies about me. He told the police that I had left him for another man and I wanted to come back to the house to live, forgetting to inform the police that I'd given Andy a letter from a solicitor for a divorce on the grounds of adultery and unreasonable behaviour. It was the police who encouraged him to change the locks.

He was clever enough to hire a private eye to get his evidence to turn the guilt around and make me the unfaithful wife and get the sympathy and support of the family and friends, and divorce me for adultery. He got away with it too.

The police arrested me for breaking and entering my own house. I was put in a cell for a few hours. I was terrified.

Andy had it all worked out. This was his way to make sure I didn't try to come back home. It happened to be Matt's eighteenth birthday: my deadline.

I found a flat, and the business paid the rent until the divorce was over and the settlement was done.

God sent me the help I needed to leave Andy – Cliff! He was the only way to stop Andy from pulling me back. He was my key to freedom.

After weeks of hell, I was at breaking point, and this was what Andy's solicitors counted on. The more difficult they were, the more I cracked under the pressure. Danny, my brother, who was a successful businessman, took over the battle for me.

When it was over, I got my divorce and came out with barely enough to buy out my siblings.

I had been in a spiritual warfare and wouldn't have made it but for the grace of God holding me up.

Just as it says in the parable, 'footsteps in the sand', I was carried though it all by God, Danny and Cliff.

Cliff kept his promise and supported me through those months, which were the most heartbreaking time of my life. I missed my home and family so much.

One day I was in my flat sitting on the sofa feeling lost and alone, when I had another vision.

I was on a train with the blinds down; I was going on a journey, not knowing where to. All I knew was there was no way back.

I was full of fear and felt the emotions of a lost five-year-old child (the age when I felt abandoned by my father).

This was a vision of my life, going on my journey not knowing where I was going. I was like a lost child.

I stayed in the relationship with Cliff for a few months. He helped me through the grief of losing my husband, family and home. Then, slowly, I let Cliff go.

I was very glad I'd met him, but knew he was sent to me just to help me get though one of the toughest times of my life. Cliff was like crutches for me to use until I was strong enough to walk on my own.

When the lease for the flat ran out, my mother let me move back into her house, on the understanding that when she passed on I would buy out my siblings.

The house was empty, and my mother had no intention of selling up, so letting me stay seemed the right thing to do.

Rosy stood back this time because Billy and Danny agreed I should have a home. After all, Rosy was in a million-pound house, Billy was settled and Danny was comfortable.

Andy was cunning enough to work on the children's emotions and got them to emotionally support him; he milked the fact that he had been betrayed.

Andy was the one with the money power. He used that to get the support from my children; he told them how much he loved them and wanted to help them buy a house of their own one day. It was as if he'd done no wrong, and got away with all the years of neglect and womanising.

I was the one who was left with the smear of the unfaithful wife.

I found it heartbreaking that my children hardly called me. I thought that they would be there for me at this time of my life when I needed them.

I lived for my children and never thought for one minute that they would desert me in my hour of need. The truth of the matter was that they were tired of the rows and fights. They wanted a normal life.

I was so caught up in my own emotional problems I couldn't see the harm that I was doing to my kids.

I was so unhappy when I left Andy, I went down to rock bottom. I thought that being free would be the answer for me. It wasn't like that at all; it was the most freighting time of my life.

I was still suffering from the trauma of the years of heart-breaks, being left with two small children when I was only twenty-three, then all the years of living with a mental disease that almost drove me to suicide.

The loss of my home, financial support, and my children was all too much for me.

I prayed, 'God, I don't have anything to live for. I have lost everything I loved. What's the point of living?'

I had some sleeping tablets in the cupboard and was seriously thinking of taking them.

Then my inner voice said, 'Kate, what about if your life was given to me?' Then I thought, OK. God, will you help me find a better life, for this one sucks! Then my inner voice said, 'I will give you a life that will be worth living, if you will trust me.'

'OK, God,' I said. 'You take over from now on…'

~24~

I had gained a lot of inner strength over the last thirty years from all the experiences I endured; I was now on the road to wisdom.

In 1993, the sleepless nights began to ease. The sobbing and heartache was subsiding. I was beginning to feel alive, once again. Little by little I was healing on the inside.

All the years of abuse and rejection, the heartbreaks and emotional pain, was slowly beginning to fade.

One morning I actually heard the birds singing and I noticed the blue sky. Spring was in the air. I took a deep breath and felt alive. I was feeling hope and energy that weren't there before. I thought, It feels like I have been given a second chance.

I couldn't help remembering the parable of the old man and the young boy who asked how to acquire wisdom.

I was someone like that young boy looking for wisdom, and there were times when I felt like I was in a deep pit where I could hardly breathe and I couldn't find my way out. Then, I felt as if a trapdoor opened, and I fell through to a place where I could breathe again.

I felt lifted from the despair and mental anguish I had for years.

I don't know if it was consciousness of God or my own mind, but I was feeling refreshed.

I had a deep desire to help others who had had their lives torn apart like mine. I wanted to make a difference in the world and help others.

Not only did leaving Andy make a phenomenal change in my life, it also caused changes in all those that were close to me. It was remarkable. It was as if a great big burden was lifted.

To give an analogy: if you could imagine a river with a big tree trunk lying across it, holding back the current of the rushing water; then suddenly, if the tree trunk was lifted, the water would just rush down that stream, taking all the debris with it. I believe that all the problems that were holding back my life when I was with Andy, also held back my family, because:

Daisy's marriage broke down.

She moved back home and worked with Andy.

Before you knew it, she was divorced and met someone new; he was a very powerful businessman.

Daisy and Andy were in his office in Sheffield at a business meeting. Andy, who was enduring a hangover from the heavy drinking the night before, said, 'Excuse the way I look, I had one too many last night.' Then he said, looking for sympathy, 'I'm going though a divorce.'

John, the businessman, said, 'Know what you mean! I'm going through a divorce myself.'

'Well, that makes three of us,' Andy said, meaning Daisy.

'Really? This calls for a celebration. How about lunch?' said John, taking a second glance at Daisy and noticing how attractive she was.

It wasn't long before Daisy and John were married, and within two years they had a baby girl. They named her Alison – my first granddaughter.

Daisy was a great support to her husband in building up their business. It was an overnight success. In no time, they built up a large enterprise worth millions.

They were in the same line of business as Andy. They manufactured orthopaedic appliances for the Ministry of Health. John supplied hospitals all over the country.

Their life was so full on with work that Alison was taken care of by one of Daisy's associates. I didn't get to see her very often because they lived too far away. I was invited up to visit from time to time.

Shelley continued her education and eventually got her degree, with honours, in art. Then she went on to get a teaching degree.

She moved to Dorset, where she got a job in a school, teaching art to A level students; it was there she met her future husband, Paul.

He came from Australia; Shelley met him on her first weekend in Dorset.

He was visiting his family and was hoping to find a wife in England. Destiny was playing its part when he met Shelley.

Missy was staying the weekend with her to help her settle in at her new apartment in Poole. 'Fancy a drink, Shelley?' said Missy after they'd unpacked.

It was a bit lively by the quayside. The pubs were packed with holidaymakers.

'Come on, Shelley, let's get a drink in the Jolly Sailor.' Missy was the brazen one and went to the bar and bought some beers.

Then in walked Paul.

Shelley looked at Missy with an expression on her face that said it all. Wow! He can't be real, he's gorgeous!

If there was love at first sight, this was it. Nature was at work. Shelley's heart missed a beat. The two of them just gazed at him and were hoping to find a way to get his attention.

Then a crowd of girls swarmed in and surrounded him. After a short while they all disappeared. They were on a hen night and took Paul with them.

The next night, Shelley and Missy went out again.

'Let's go to the pub and see if that gorgeous guy is there,' Missy suggested.

Off they went. It was a lovely warm evening in early September, and the nightlife was just beginning.

The two girls went in and bought a beer, sat down and watched the door intently. They finished their drink, waited for about half an hour, and then, with a feeling of disappointment, got up and went out. But as soon as they stepped outside, Paul turned up and went inside the pub.

Shelley said to Missy, 'What do we do now?'

'We go back in!'

They went back, and Shelley sat down while Missy went to the bar. She went straight up to Paul and said, 'Hi, we saw you in here last night. Would you like to join us for a drink?'

'Sure,' he said, and sat down next to Shelley.

He put his arm over the armchair Shelley was sitting in. That was the start of a true romance that took Shelley to live in Australia.

She worked through her contract with the school first and got married to Paul a year later.

Missy met the love of her life at Luton Airport.

She was on her way with Daisy and Shelley to Tenerife for a week's holiday. Happy to be getting away with her sisters for a bit of fun, Missy suddenly recognised a boy she knew very well. He was booking seats on the same flight.

'Hi, Gary, what you doing here?' Missy said.

Gary replied with a big grin on his face, 'Hello! Fancy seeing you here. Are you getting on this flight?'

'Yeah, we're going to Tenerife,'

'So are we. Where are you staying?'

'Don't know yet – we're gonna find a place when we get there.'

Gary was with two of his mates.

Well, you can only guess where they ended up: with the girls in their villa. They stayed a few days until they found a place of their own.

That was true romance for Missy. Gary was the one for her, fun-loving and carefree. They were made for each other.

Matt became a writer; he also learned to play the guitar and wrote his own music. Within no time he'd formed his own band; he was the lead singer.

Matt grew into a tall, very tall young man, and his build matched his height. When he walked into a room all heads turned. Not only was he tall and handsome, he had the charisma of a superstar.

I saw my son performing one night and was so proud of him. He reminded me of Elvis Presley.

Matt caught my eye as he was doing his thing and gave me a smile as if to say, 'This is your son, Mum!

The band was simply the best. They were all very talented musicians.

I do believe that Matt was born to be a musician. At the age of three, he loved to listen to the audio tape that I played in my car. His favourite track was 'Jesus Christ Superstar'. Matt was in a world of his own when he was performing.

My family got on with living their own lives in no time.

I had better start living mine, I told myself.

I thought if I want to change the world I'd better get some help, so I decided to start with the twelve step recovery programme.

First of all I had to get a sponsor – that's a person who practises the programme themselves. He or she gives guidance through sharing, listening, explaining the programme and pointing out the choices available.

These kinds of people were hard to find, as most of the people in the meetings were looking for help, just like me. I got my strength from identifying with them.

When they spoke about how their partner, wife, husband, child or friend changed when they drank or took drugs, I identified with how it affected them.

The reason I kept going back to those meetings was because they all knew what it was like when their loved one changed, like a Jekyll and Hyde personality, into someone who insulted them and attacked them emotionally, mentally and sometimes physically.

I was given hope at those meetings to find a way to cope with this disease and make a better life for myself.

Now that I was no longer living with Andy, I could work the programme that they talked about.

There are only a few people who can work this programme while still in a relationship with their partner. Their partner needs to be on a programme of recovery as well. In other words, the mental disease, which I choose to call it, has to be arrested. Very few people can get better while in a relationship with an active addict.

The experiences I had while living with this 'mental disease' gave me the wisdom of knowing how it works. It's very cunning, and somehow knows when and where to attack. Only those who have lived with this kind of affliction will understand what I'm talking about.

I found myself a sponsor and began with step one.

'We admitted we were powerless over alcohol; that our lives have become unmanageable.'[1]

---

[1] 'Step One' from *Alcoholics Anonymous*, Alcoholics Anonymous World Services, Inc, p59

'OK, Kate,' said Jessie, my sponsor. She was a lady who had being around the programme for many years. She was caring and wise. She was a little stout, with black hair that she backcombed to make it stand up a little, and she wore large glamorous earrings.

Jessie was something like a goth in some ways. She wore black most of the time.

When you were in her presence you couldn't help feeling light and happy. There was something special about Jessie that gave you a feeling that she really cared about your welfare.

'I want you to write down all the things that you feel you are powerless over, going back as far as you can remember,' Jessie said.

She gave me a sheet of paper and I got to work writing down everything that I could remember that I was powerless over.

I looked back to the time when I was five years old and I wanted my father to pick me up and put me on his knee and tell me how much he missed me and that he loved me.

I was powerless over the fact that he didn't show any love and affection.

I wrote how powerless I was over my mother not showing the same love and respect to me as she did towards my sister.

I wrote about my sister's rejection of me.

Then there was the rejection I had from my in-laws and so-called friends. I wrote down all I could remember in order to understand my powerlessness over them.

I also wrote down how powerless I was when I went through my divorce, and how I was cheated of my financial rights.

The last thing that I wrote was how powerless I was over Andy's drinking.

The amount of time and energy I'd spent trying to get him to stop drinking... I could have gone on and on. But the idea was to understand how we were powerless over people, not to dwell on the past.

The next time I met up with my sponsor, I read out all that I wrote.

Jessie said, 'As we look back on our lives, we acknowledge our powerlessness over every person and event where we sought for control over other people, their actions and their addiction.

'An enormous burden is lifted when you accept your powerlessness. Then you will discover freedom and the power you do have to define and live your own life.'

Jessie gave me a list of questions for self-study to take home. I worked on this list with a willing heart.

Once I'd accepted my powerlessness over people, places and things, I let go of the struggle to try to change things that didn't go my way.

Jessie was right. It was as if a heavy burden was lifted. I was doing all right but had to find a way to earn a living.

It was amazing how Rosy made money. She advertised lucky charms and sold them to people who believed in that sort of thing. So, I became one of the workers Rosy employed.

My mother helped out now and then, but she was getting old now, so most of the time she made the tea and cooked the meals.

Rosy's two children were on the team of workers too. The mail order business built up to be quite a successful enterprise.

It wasn't easy being humble to Rosy. At times I felt as if I was in a Cinderella syndrome. I was treated like someone who was less than the rest.

I used one of the slogans from my programme – 'Just for today' – and the serenity prayer: 'God, give me the serenity to accept the things I cannot change, courage to change the things I can and the wisdom to know the difference.'[2] We, the members, call these self-help slogans and prayers our tools, so to speak.

I waited until I was ready to become well enough to move on.

I had no qualification for being employed by anyone except in a factory, working as a machinist. I couldn't revert back to that hard work, so I chose to be with my family and eat humble pie. Rosy paid me well.

The conversations I had with God were clearly becoming more and more fluent.

It was as if God was my best friend. We often chatted about the future and what my next thought should be. My wisdom was developing enough to understand how my thinking affected my future.

---

[2] 'The Serenity Prayer' from *Twelve Steps and Twelve Traditions*, Alcoholics Anonymous World Services, Inc, p42

I had to be diligent with my settlement money, as there wasn't any pension set up for me. I left all those things with Andy to sort out, and it didn't go in my favour.

I used some of my settlement money to set up a pension for when I retired, and I needed to have enough to buy out my siblings when the house was ready to be sold.

Fortunately for me, I was to inherit a fourth of the property, so this made it possible for me to afford to buy the house in the future.

Step one helped me to accept my powerlessness over my financial and work situation.

The little three-bedroom council house I now lived in under the rules of my mother was in need of repair and decorating.

The window frames were made from iron. The door had a crack in it. On a windy day, the draught would come whizzing through, making an eerie wind sound and causing cold air to blow through the house.

There wasn't any central heating. The electric wiring was in need of repair. The place was cold and empty.

I asked my companion, whom I called God, 'How am I going to get all this done, and how am I going to find the money?'

My mind spoke to me, 'Kate, life states that as you sow, so shall you reap.'

This gave me food for thought.

This house is the reflection of how I have lived in the past. It's dead; there isn't any life in it. No one has lived in it for years. It's cold and empty. Yes! This cold dead house is reflecting *me*. I was dead and empty. My spiritual life was dying; this house is mirroring me, it's showing me who I am and what I've done to myself.

I thought, I'm going to make this house come back to life; I'm going to come back to life. This house will reflect my recovery. As I get better, so shall this house. I will paint it, repair it and most of all, I will love it.

~25~

I decided to work in the garden as my first task, mainly because my mother didn't want me to change things in the house. So I started to dig the garden.

The ground was hard and solid. The earth was like rock. It took a lot of hard work, breaking it and turning it over. The garden was massive. You could have built another house on the land that surrounded the house.

Digging the hard ground and turning it over to plant new seeds reflected how I was now breaking the old thought patterns that had created my past experiences. My thinking had to change. New thoughts had to be planted to create a better future.

I worked hard digging the earth and turning it over.

When I finished I planted one hundred rose bushes, all because someone said when I left Andy, 'She's left a bed of roses, leaving her husband.' I thought, I'll make my own bed of roses. That's why I planted so many bushes. Plus the earth was mostly clay, and roses like clay, as it holds the water.

I visited my sponsor again and spent the evening talking about how to change the future by learning to think differently.

She told me how she worked on changing her own thought patterns.

'Kate, you can change your life, beginning with just a thought,' she said. 'It's those old thought patterns that created the past and led you to where you are today. If you don't change them you will create much of the same.'

All I had to do was change my thinking. I learned that my mind was controlling my life. Jessie said, 'A thought is energy, and the universe doesn't judge what we think. It just obeys our thoughts.'

I answered, 'We're not what we think we are, but we are what we think.'

Jessie smiled and said, 'You're getting it, Kate.'

I learned that if we're negative in our thinking and become anxious, fearful, confused and angry, we create a great deal of adrenaline in our bodies. This in turn increases heart rate and blood pressure. Then we create the very thing we are afraid of, simply because the mind is focusing on what we are thinking. Therefore, I realised, I was the creator of my own reality.

All this new-found knowledge made sense to me. So I set to work on becoming conscious of my thinking. This wasn't easy, because my mind patterns went way back. They were hard to control. It was like trying to control the wind.

'Try affirmations,' said Jessie. 'Here are a few:

I am whole and complete in myself.

I love and appreciate myself just as I am.

I am an open channel of creative energy.

All things are now working together for good in my life.

'These are only a few to start with. Try out the ones you feel comfortable with. You write them down three times in the present tense, such as:

I, Kate, am now an open channel of creative energy.

I, Kate, am now an open channel of creative energy.

I, Kate, am now an open channel of creative energy.

'Then write like you are someone outside of you agreeing with you:

Kate, you are now an open channel of creative energy.

Kate, you are now an open channel of creative energy.

Kate, you are now an open channel of creative energy.

'Then write as if there is a crowd of people speaking to you. If you like, you can visualise yourself on a platform with people cheering you:

Kate is an open channel of creative energy.

Kate is an open channel of creative energy.

Kate is an open channel of creative energy.

'Then you write, "This or something better is now manifesting in my life for the highest good of all concerned."

'Do these twice a day, first thing in the morning or last thing at night, for two weeks. You can choose more affirmations if you want to, but no more than three at a time.'

I did this and worked towards my recovery with determination to find out what else the twelve steps had to offer me.

After a while, I was ready for the next step – 'step two': 'Came to believe that a power greater than ourselves could restore us to sanity.'[3]

'Are you ready to work your second step now, Kate?' Jessie said.

'Yes I am, but I feel that I do believe in a power greater than myself already. I think that this power has got me thought the rough ride life has given me and led me here.

'But I have to wonder why this step says "restore us to sanity". Is this implying I'm insane?' I said, puzzled at the implication of being insane.

Jessie said, 'How many times did you believe that your husband would change when you forgave him for his unacceptable behaviour? How many times did you tell yourself, "I'm leaving" and didn't go? What about the rows you had and the things you said in temper? One minute you hated him, then the next you loved him. How about the times you went to a solicitor for a divorce? And how many times did you tell your children you were going to leave him, but didn't go?'

'Erm, yes, I guess you're right, Jessie. It was very insane behaviour.'

'There you go, Kate! Now is the time for you to let the past go and forgive all those who harmed you.' She paused.

'Step two is about "coming" to believe that there's a power

---

[3] 'Step Two' from *Alcoholics Anonymous*, Alcoholics Anonymous World Services, Inc, p59

greater than us that can restore us to sanity. You see, Kate, there are some people who don't believe in God because they've had such a hard time in their life. They say, "How can there be a God when there is so much hardship and pain?" Or there are some that have had a religious God, which has turned them away from any form of belief. This step is for those who need to find a higher power. That can be anything. For some people, it's the meetings. It isn't organised religion. It's simply a power greater than you are. It can be Jesus for those who believe in him or it could be Buddha. It really doesn't matter, just as long as you believe that there is a power greater than you.'

Jessie went on to say, 'This power greater than you, I like to think, is deep within us, waiting for us to wake up and become conscious of it – plug in, so to speak.

'You can't get the lights to work in the house if you don't turn on the switch, can you? Imagine yourself hoovering the floor without being plugged in. You can see the Hoover, you know that it's there, but without turning it on, it's powerless.'

I listened and thought, I don't have to come to believe, I *do* believe. But I understood that this step wasn't just for me, it was for all those who wanted to work them.

I know that there is a higher power because of all I have to do is look at life: the abundance of nature, the way things evolve. The universe and planets are all working in harmony, keeping the world turning and nourished.

Jessie said, 'Life is like an orchestra. Each one of us playing our part to make this a wonderful world to experience, but when we separate ourselves from the Master and go our own way, we play out of tune. To get back into harmony, we need to know who we are and where we come from.'

She went on to say, 'The entire twelve steps are suggestions.[4] All you need is an open mind and the steps will gradually infiltrate your life.

'True humility and having an open mind can lead you to faith and assurance that God (of your understanding) will restore you to sanity.

---

[4] *Twelve Steps and Twelve Traditions*, Alcoholics Anonymous World Services, Inc, p26

'If we rightly relate ourselves to God, then the grace of God can enter us and expel the obsessions.' This for me meant being obsessed with Andy's drinking problem.

I said, 'There are all sorts of things people are obsessed with – drink, food, sex, and many more things that cause us humans to become out of harmony with God's will. My obsession is to want a happy family life.'

'Kate, we need to take a look at ourselves in a deep and meaningful way – to clean our house, so to speak. We have to forgive all those who have harmed us, and make amends to all those that we have harmed.'

'So I have to forgive all those who hurt me, and make amends to them?'

'All the insanity didn't just belong exclusively to the person who drank – whether spouse, parent, child or friend. We have to come to believe that we too need to change.'

'But how can I think about making amends to Andy when he did so much harm to me?' I asked.

'We are often distorted by anger, frustration and fear. This programme is centred on us; our behaviour needs to be questioned.'

I was learning quite a lot from Jessie and wanted to take it all in, so I had to stop and evaluate all that she was saying.

'So I have to believe in a power greater that me and accept its guidance because I can't work alone?'

Jessie answered, 'I know that my human will and wisdom works in the dark, and there is so much I need to know about myself and about others. Taking the second step suggests that our human experience and intelligence isn't enough, and we're not alone and we need more than ourselves to solve the problems.'

Jessie was getting a lot of her wisdom from the literature she obtained at the meeting she went to. She went on to say, 'We are all equals, but not all the same. It's so important to find one's own way, to try and respect other people's beliefs or doubts. All you have to do is believe in a power greater than yourself and to be willing to forgive. Nothing more is required from you to make your beginning.'

I loved listening to what Jessie said about a 'higher power' and how to bring this power to work in my life.

One day I decided to prune the trees in my garden; they were a bit wild.

Out came the wood saw and I got sawing away at the branches of the pear trees. When I'd finished I stood back and thought, oh, dear, I think I have taken too much off. The poor tree looked very bare. Then I heard my inner voice again.

'That's what I have done to you, Kate. Cut everything away from you. The trees will bring forth new and stronger branches next year that will bare healthy fruit.'

Yes, I thought how empty I felt when I left Andy. I really did feel stripped of all I had, just like the pear trees. But now I know I am growing stronger and wiser…

I now used my new understanding of the higher power to help me change my situation with my earnings.

I knew it wasn't good for me to work for Rosy. I felt suppressed, even though I was very grateful for the opportunity to earn money. I thought, What can I do to be independent and earn some money? What am I good at? Erm, sewing? No, that doesn't work, I've tried that.

I started to make curtains. I advertised in the local newspaper. I got some work, but I was expected to put up the curtains as well as make them and some of the rails were in need of fixing. I wasn't earning enough for all that and gave up after a while.

Then I tried caring for the elderly.

I found myself travelling on an icy motorway at ten o'clock at night to put an old lady to bed and was only paid £2. I thought, What I am doing? Then the agency I was working for offered me a job caring for a baby who was severely handicapped.

He was paralysed from the waist down and was brain damaged.

The mother of the baby took a liking to me, so I took the job, but it didn't pay enough.

Meanwhile, I thought again, I've looked after a family for the last twenty years. I'm very experienced at taking care of children and I miss my family so much. Maybe I could foster.

In 1994, I was accepted as a teenage foster-parent, after weeks of meetings and form-filling. I really had my heart in it and eventually I was able to give up working for Rosy; or to put it another way, Rosy sacked me because I was late coming in one morning.

It was just before Christmas. I didn't have any money that Christmas, but I trusted in my higher power to take care of me.

My first foster-child came to stay with me just after Christmas.

He was a lovely black boy from Uganda. He was so happy with me he didn't want to leave when it was time for him to go.

I had found my vocation. Fostering was for me, and it paid well.

I fostered quite a few teenagers and was a good foster-parent.

At last I was financially solvent, independent, and my confidence was growing.

Jessie was always there for me when I found life tough, and the meetings were a great support too.

~26~

The next step was 'step three': 'Made a decision to turn our will and our lives over to the care of God, as we understood Him.'[5]

'Jessie,' I said, 'I'm ready for step three now. Where do I begin?'

'This is a very important step, Kate; there aren't any half measures.'

'That's OK; I've already given my life over to the care of God. I would like to do it again with you.'

'OK, let's begin. The first phrase of step three is "Make a decision". This means that we have choices. Everyone has their own pace for working these steps. Not many of us are able to immediately turn over everything in our lives; making the decision to do so is a commitment to try.'

'I've heard it said, Jessie, that to be willing is the key that opens the door.'

'That's right, Kate. Then we face the question of how shall we do it once we have the key of willingness and place it in the lock. What do you do next?'

'Don't know. Do tell me.'

'You take one problem or person at a time, then turn that thing over to your higher power and try to bring your will into agreement with God's intention for you. This is the purpose of the twelve steps, and step three opens the door.' Jessie went on to say, 'We are all free to decide how we will communicate with our higher power. You could start and end the day with the serenity prayer, or ask directly for God to take your will and life for that day.'

I thought I'd ask God to help me to do His will in my life on a daily basis.

'Have you any questions, Kate?' Jessie asked me.

---

[5] *Alcoholics Anonymous*, Alcoholics Anonymous World Services, Inc, p59

'I don't think so. I am willing to do this step, and I will start by asking God to help me with the problem I have with my children. They never call me, and they seem to be more interested in Andy than calling their mother. I feel angry with them; they know how he treated me. My son Matt is the only one who comes to see me now. He's having a hard time with his father, because Andy brought his mistress to live in the house.

'He might have to stay with me. It's tough on him, as my place is in need of repair and doesn't have any central heating. Matt isn't used to this. He has a lovely room at home, a swimming pool and the luxuries of a bathroom en suite. He is a lost soul at the moment.'

'Let go of your son and ask your higher power to take care of his needs. As for your other children, say the serenity prayer in the morning and when you go to bed. Do this for a few days and see what the outcome will be,' Jessie suggested. 'If we trust and stay close to God and ask Him to take care of us and in return we try to perform His work, we will find ourselves becoming less and less interested in ourselves, and more and more we'll become interested in seeing what we can contribute to life.'

'That's why I'm here, Jessie. I want a better life and I'm willing to go to any lengths.'

'With this new power, you will have peace of mind and will lose your fear and discover you can have a happy and successful life,' Jessie said.

I learned the serenity prayer.

'God grant me the serenity to accept the things I can't change, change the things I can and have the wisdom to know the difference.' I did what Jessie suggested, and prayed night and morning to invite my God to take over my life and do His will.

After a few days I felt better about my children, and Matt moved in with me until he found a flat of his own.

Matt was a very angry man. He didn't speak to his father for a very long time. He was also angry with me, and when he got his own flat he detached himself from me for many years.

As for my other children, Daisy was in her own world of success.

Shelley was with the new man in her life.

Missy was her father's blue-eyed daughter. They were

inseparable. I was grateful for that. At least one of my daughters had a father's love.

I did find it hard to accept that all my children had detached themselves from me.

It was a horrible feeling, finding that one moment I was surrounded by my family and the next I was on my own.

I did wish them all well, and used step three to help me let go and try to do 'God's will'.

The programme was working; I began to lose interest in myself and began to contribute to life.

Fostering teenagers helped me through this time of grieving for the loss of my family life.

All my expectations and my vision of a happy family life were gone. It took many tears and a lot of pain, but slowly I let go of the past.

The garden was a healthy hobby. It brought me close to the God of my understanding, which was my companion who spoke to me in my own voice.

I had a new pathway made, because it was muddy walking from the car to the door. This symbolised the new path I was on, the path to recovery.

So many times God spoke to me during those years in my garden.

I'm ready to do the fourth step now, I thought.

'Hi, Jessie. Can I come over to start work on my fourth step when you're free?' I said on the phone.

'Sure, lovely. How about Monday evening about seven?'

'I'll be there.'

Step four: 'Made a searching and fearless moral inventory of ourselves.'[6]

'Now, this task is to deal with the difficult issues of your life, past and present,' said Jessie.

'If you hide from the truth, nothing will be solved. In blaming others, justifying and rationalising your actions for all the problems in your life, you'll never find serenity. Remember, Kate, you are only asked to take an inventory, not to do anything about what you learn.'

'What's it all about, Jessie, an inventory?'

---

[6] *Alcoholics Anonymous*, Alcoholics Anonymous World Services, Inc, p59

'It's a kind of personal house cleaning, a strenuous effort to face and to be rid of things in ourselves which have been blocking us. A personal, fearless moral inventory.

'First we search for the flaws in our own make-up. *Resentment* is said to be the number one offender. It destroys more people than anything else does.[7] These resentments must be mastered.'

'But how?' I asked.

'We realise that the people who wronged us were maybe spiritually sick – they, like ourselves, were sick too. So we ask God to help us, by asking God to show them the same patience, tolerance, and pity that we would have for a sick friend.'

'So what you're saying, Jessie, is, I am just as sick as all those that harmed me.'

'I'm saying, Kate, that this step is about your inventory. It's about looking inside yourself so that you can see how you were affected by those who have this mental disease.

'The injuries that caused your life to be dysfunctional were caused not only by the drinker, but your childhood experiences, parents, siblings and teachers – the people who were close to you and used you to feed their disease.'

Jessie was on a roll and continued, 'The resentment and anger that we have is stuck inside us, they are blocking us from the light of knowing who we really are.

'This step is asking us to take responsibility for the part *we* played; to look at the way we reacted to the offender. The unconscious thoughts, the things we said in response to this illness.

'Resentment and anger can cause all sorts of problems for us. It leaves inside us shadows of negative energy that get stuck in our bodies.'

'Where do we begin then, Jessie?'

'We make a list of all those we hold a grudge against.'

I had a puzzled look on my face. Jessie smiled and said, 'Don't worry, Kate, it's not something you can't handle. Remember, we want to keep it simple.

'A "grudge list" is a simple way of finding out how we were injured by all those who hurt us and how we reacted to our

---

[7] *Alcoholics Anonymous*, Alcoholics Anonymous World Services, Inc, p64

injury, how it affected us and what our part in it was. Also, it will help you to work out your shortcomings that stand in the way of you becoming one with yourself, the universe and God.'[8]

'Sounds like a lot of work, Jessie! There are so many people who I have a grudge against. But what puzzles me is I can't see what my part is in all this. What did I do? I was the one who stayed at home with my children while my husband was out enjoying his life. I was the one my father didn't show love to – and what about my children? Why do they show more affection to Andy, when he wasn't emotionally there for them and I was?'

'Exactly, Kate; that's why you hold resentments. They come from your injuries. When you have done the first, second and third steps, briefly you say, "I can't, God can, I let him." I believe you can't do the fourth step until you have done the first three steps.'

'Why?' I said.

'Because God knows what's blocking you, and only God can set you free if you have the right thinking. Tell you what, Kate, let's see this in another light. Take the computer. If you know how a computer works you will know that you need a PC guard. If you don't have one you get viruses that can block you from the power to connect to the network.

'If you get a virus, you use the power of the PC guard to delete the virus. It disappears in seconds when the right command is given.

'So it is with the resentments that are inside you. They are blocking you from the light of God, and stopping you from living the life that you were born to live.

'If you understand how the twelve steps work, you can delete the resentments and any other form of unhealthy thoughts that have affected you. Then you use your higher power to keep you free from future defects. He becomes your PC guard, so to speak.'

I thought about this and was willing to see what my defects were.

'Now let's say a little prayer before we begin, Kate.' Jessie read out the step-three prayer from the AA book. ' "God, I offer myself to Thee, to build with me and to do with me Thou wilt. Relieve

---

[8] *Alcoholics Anonymous*, Alcoholics Anonymous World Services, Inc, p65

me of the bondage of self, that I may better do Thy will. Take away my difficulties, that victory over them may bear witness to those I would help of Thy power, Thy love and Thy way of life. May I do Thy will always. Amen." '[9]

Then she showed me how to do a grudge list.

'First of all, write down the persons whom you hold a grudge against e.g. husbands, father, father-in-law, mother, mother-in-law, sister, sister-in-law, children, teacher, and friend.

'Write what they did to cause you to have a grudge. Then write down how this affected your life. This is defined in five areas: emotional, physical, sexual, spiritual, and intellectual.

'When you have done that, write down what your part was in it. In other words, how did you react?

'Here is a list of co-dependant behaviours with each person throughout each relationship. Specific behaviours may be difficult to remember. Our behaviours could have included these:

Lying, manipulating, raging, judging, avoiding, over-controlling, denying, abusing, offending

Passiveness, neglecting, punishing, discounting, aggressive-ness, silence, victimising, distancing

Abandoning, over-pleasing, shaming, teasing, helplessness, bitterness, enmeshing, hating and resenting.

'Tick the ones that come into your mind when you look at the injuries that you had.

'If you are humble and honest you can see where you have been selfish, dishonest, self-seeking and frightened through a situation that has not been entirely your fault. Then you try to disregard the other person involved, because the inventory is yours, not the other person's.'

I looked at my part in all this and understood that it was necessary to keep my side of the street clean, no matter what anyone else did to me. This was a hard thing to do because reminding me of all my injuries was like opening up a can of worms...

The past experiences that affected my life in a deep and

[9] *Alcoholics Anonymous*, Alcoholics Anonymous World Services, Inc, p63

painful way were highlighted.

The anger and resentment welled up inside me so much. You could say I felt as if I had a fire in my belly; or to put it another way, a volcano that was ready to erupt. I couldn't get past it. I had a long way to go before I could come to the place in my life where I could forgive.

'Jessie, this step is tough. It's waking up in me all the pain of the past, going back to my childhood,' I said.

'That's the idea, Kate. When you feel the anger and resentment, it's then you make a choice. You either hold onto the anger and blame, or you choose to ask God to help you understand that they were sick, and to give you the spirit of forgiveness towards all those who wronged you.'

'I do have so much anger, I'm so angry with my father, mother, Andy, his sister, Andy's mother and father, Rob and his lover, Rosy. I feel such a victim.'

'Yes, I know, Kate, tell me how does that make you feel?'

'Real bad, Jessie.'

'Now is the time to expose all those feelings and to bring them into the light for God to heal you. I know it's painful. Remember, "No pain, no gain". This is how God works, Kate; you have to feel the pain in order for God to heal. When you change your thinking, with the help of your higher power, you will find in yourself a sense of being worthwhile and usefulness to God and others. All you have to do is change your thinking and your attitude and – most of all – be willing to forgive. When you let go of the past, the universe will then work towards the power of intention, Things in your favour will come to you. Then the world acts as an outside mirror to what's on the inside, and then you can make goals for a better future.'

I went home that night with my head full of my fourth step. I identified with many of the shortcomings on the list, and wanted to take responsibility for my part in all the dysfunctional behaviour I had experienced over the past years. But I wasn't ready to move on as I hoped to.

The rage inside me wouldn't go when I asked God to take it away. I prayed for all those who had harmed me, but I knew that the resentments were still there.

I stayed on this plateau for a number of years. All I could do was be willing for God to take away my defect of character. I got on with my life, wanting to get better and to forgive. But it had to be in God's time. Jessie was planning to move to the north and told me she wouldn't be around to work the rest of the steps with me.

'I'm sorry, Kate, but this is as far as I can take you. I will be moving in two weeks. You can call me anytime for a chat if you want. I just want to say, I enjoyed working with you. I got so much out of our time together. I have a gift for you; it's one of my favourite books – *The Road Less Travelled* by M Scott Peck. Take care... I love you.'

I was sad to say goodbye to Jessie and thought, I will have to find another sponsor to help me work the next step.

~27~

Two years passed. I was now fifty-six. I didn't find another sponsor. There wasn't anyone who could live up to Jessie as far as I was concerned.

The book Jessie gave me was one of the most enlightening books I'd read. I read it and reread it. It taught me many things about life.

One was: when two people meet, they fall crazily in love. At least that's what they think they are – 'in love'. Little do they know that it's nature at work.

The universe plays tricks on us. It's basically all about sex. When two people meet and have eye contact, the signals are sent to the brain and then all the hormones get to work. The next thing to sex is touch. Once the couple touch each other, nature takes over and gives them the desire to make love. All this sexual attraction is for the purpose of evolution. They can't leave each other alone. They think that they will be in love for ever. Then as time goes by, the sexual attraction fades. That's when they can either make a choice to love each other, or move on to the next person for that loved-up feeling again. M Scott Peck says, 'Love is not a feeling, it's a choice.'

Nothing stays the same. People change, and if you haven't learned to love yourself you can't love others. This is because you will be looking for someone to love you, to fill that empty space that must be filled by yourself and God.

When you have learned to love yourself, God's love will be flowing from you to others and expect nothing in return.

No matter how hard I tried, I couldn't get the rage to leave me. In fact, every time I prayed for God to take away the anger, the more the anger rose. It felt like the anger was speaking to me, saying, 'I'm not going; I've been here for years!'

The 'stinking thinking' was the mental disease at work. It said, 'I'm staying; they cheated you from your money, your children, the business, your house!'

For as long as I had this anger and resentment, I was a prisoner of this mental disease.

It didn't help when I heard that Andy had met someone else and she'd moved into my family home.

No, I wasn't able to let go, no matter how much I tried to.

The mental disease was active in my head. I believed it was my mind speaking to me. I wasn't conscious of the difference between my thinking and the mental disease at that time. It really was a form of insanity. All I knew was it wasn't from a good source; it was from the dark side of life.

At last, my mother let me put central heating in at the house, and I had the electric wiring replaced.

I had this belief that when I did a profound and positive action in my life, the outside reflected it... (The world acts as an outside mirror to what's on the inside.)

I believed that the central heating and electric wiring was reflecting the higher power I invited into my life when I did step three.

My inner voice spoke to me again. It said, 'You are now connected to the source, Kate. All you have to do is have faith.'

I understood that 'faith' was what turns on the power.

The next thing that I needed to work on in the house was to decorate the rooms; but then my mother became sick. She suffered a heart attack.

All the family was called to the hospital. The surgeons fought for her life that day. The team was wonderful; they worked so hard to keep her alive.

Every time her heart stopped they brought her back. Mum wasn't going anywhere just yet.

She said to Rosy, 'Get me out of here, Rosy; they keep hitting me with a hammer!'

She had a wonderful sense of humour. The hammer that she thought they were hitting her with was the machine that got her heart to beat again.

From then on I spent a lot of time helping Rosy to look after my sick mother. The heart attack she had left her with a disorder that caused her to suffer from a nervous disposition, for which she needed to take tranquillisers.

Then she became addicted to them. She suffered for a further three years. But God was good; Mum wanted to go to Shelley's wedding. So her willpower kept her going so that her wish could come true.

Paul's father came over from Australia for the wedding, and when he set eyes on me, he was smitten and was quick to tell me.

'Hi, I'm Oscar. Pleased to meet you,' he said, holding out his hand to shake mine. He didn't have an Australian accent; in fact he spoke like an aristocrat.

Oscar was an educated man and spoke four languages. He originally came from Denmark. He had the bluest eyes I'd had ever seen. His hair was white and had probably been blond in his younger days. He was a tall man, a bit overweight, but very charming and good-looking. I loved the way he was so polite. His posh accent was endearing.

'Hello, how are you?' I said, smiling. I looked pretty good in my floral dress. Although I was ageing, I still looked much younger than my years.

The wedding was a happy day. Shelley wore a simple long white dress. It was a Laura Ashley designer dress. The wedding reception was in a yacht club overlooking the sea.

Oscar couldn't take his eyes of me the whole time we were together.

Rosy came with my mother, knowing that this was probably the last opportunity for Mum to be at a family wedding. She was very frail by then and needed a lot of attention. Rosy was quick in getting me to do my part to look after our mother.

It was typical of my mother to attract attention as often as she could, so I wasn't surprised when she decided she needed to go to the bathroom just as the wedding was about to begin.

'Where's Mum?' Shelley said.

'Don't know, the last time I saw her she was with Rosy and your nan,' Paul replied.

I was in the toilet, helping my mother to sort herself out with unmentionable problems. I said, 'I'm sorry, Rosy, I really must leave Mum with you. I'm late. I'm a witness; they will be wondering where I am.'

Rosy was a bit tense with it all; she was the main carer for my mother and found it all too much at times.

In fact Rosy was pretty angry that she was in this position. She felt trapped by the twenty-four-hour care she had to give to her mother, and that anger was aimed at me more often than not.

I got to the register office just in time for the wedding to begin. I was so proud of my daughter that day. She looked a picture, with her very dark brown hair tied back in a French plait and cornflowers woven in and around her hair.

Cornflowers are Shelley's favourite flowers; the reception room was decorated everywhere with them.

Unfortunately, though, I didn't get to see the disco party in the evening; I drank too much wine at the reception. Not only that, I had Pimm's Number One in the pub before the wedding. That was a drink based on gin with all sorts of other additives.

Rosy likes a Pimm's Number One, and she bought one for me. It looked harmless, decorated with fruit and cucumber, but it was quite potent. In fact, I drank two, not realising how strong they were. Added to the wine I had with dinner, it was more than I could take. I was sick and spent the whole evening in bed.

I stayed in Shelley's flat that night. Oscar slept on the floor in the living room.

The next day, the two of us were on our own. Then Oscar just couldn't keep his emotions concealed any more. He had to blurt it out, 'Kate, I think you're gorgeous! I do believe we could make a go of it. I've been on my own for too many years. I think you would love it in Sydney. What do you think?'

My mind was working overtime. I thought, Wouldn't it be great if I could start a new life in Australia. I thought long and hard, but I noticed that Oscar drank a lot. (Not that I could be the judge about drinking that evening!)

The rumour was he was an alcoholic.

'I'm flattered, Oscar, that you made me this offer.' (I thought, I can't live with another heavy drinker.) 'But I have my family here, and I will miss them.'

The truth was I was lonely; my children had their own lives to live. The thought of going did cross my mind. This man had his own house, and I wouldn't have any money worries. I didn't have a very happy life here; maybe it could be an option. I couldn't decide anything, so I let it go. They say, when in doubt, do nought.

I took Oscar to the airport and saw him off on his journey back to Oz.

'I do hope you think about it, Kate,' he said.

'The thing is, Oscar, I've been married to a man who drank a lot, and I feel you like a drink too.'

'I only drink because I'm on my own. It helps the loneliness. If you were in my life I wouldn't need to drink,' he said with a look of pleading. I thought, I can't take the risk.

I smiled and said, 'Maybe.'

But I wasn't going straight from the frying pan into the fire by getting involved with another drinker.

A few months after Shelley's wedding, my mother passed away.

She came from the backstreets of London and was a hard worker. She brought her children through a war and worked her way through the aftermath.

My mother was a strong and powerful lady. No one controlled her; she was the boss of our family and yes, even Rosy depended on her.

All her children loved and respected her, whether she was right or wrong. She was the queen bee, so to speak.

Rosy took her home to live with her after my father died; she took care of her and made sure she didn't want for anything. Rosy had the money to take her on many holidays, cruising the Mediterranean and the Caribbean Sea. Yes, my mother had a wonderful, full life, up until the last seven years.

Her illness proved to be the hardest battle she ever had. How she suffered!

The first heart attack she had was major. The doctors were amazed that she got over it and had a full recovery. Then came the second heart attack, where she was brought back nine times. It left her with a severe nervous condition.

Her addiction to the little blue pill (Arazapan) turned her into an addict that was painful to see and to live with.

Her condition gave me a sadness that turned all the resentment and anger from the past into compassion. All the anger that I had towards my mother disappeared.

All I felt in my heart when my mother died was love. It must have come from a spiritual place. I was blessed, because I saw my mother for the person she really was: a kind, thoughtful, generous lady who loved me and was the best storyteller in the world – that is, as far as I was concerned.

I remembered the time when I was a small child, looking into the fire and waiting for the stories I loved to hear my mother tell.

She left an empty space inside me when she went. It was like a light had gone out.

Her coffin was covered in roses.

The sadness I had when she was cremated gave me the desire for someone to hold me and love me. Maybe I should find someone to fill this empty space. I thought.

Oscar wrote to me when he heard about my mother's death. He tried to persuade me to come to Sydney and have a relationship with him. He wouldn't let it go. I wrote back and said, 'I'll think about it if you are prepared to give up drinking.'

The thought of running away to Australia began to get a hold of me. I reminded myself that Missy spent most of her time with Andy. Daisy lived miles away in Sheffield, and was too busy to call. Matt needed his own space to find himself. He was busy with his band. I was a bit of a lost soul at that time; the loneliness was more than I could bear.

The phone calls from Oscar saying how I would be happy with him kept coming.

I decided to take a trip to Australia anyway. The money I had left over from my settlement after I had bought out my siblings to purchase my mother's house was enough to pay for the flight.

There was another reason why I wanted to go to Australia. Shelley had a baby. I wanted to meet my new granddaughter.

The trip was a real challenge for me. I was so afraid to travel all that way on my own. I was trembling in my shoes the day I got on that flight all by myself.

I was afraid of getting lost in Singapore, where I did the transfer. Suppose I can't find the gateway, I thought. I was petrified. It took all my courage to get on that plane.

When I eventually arrived, Shelley, Paul and her baby,

Isabelle, were waiting to meet me. Oscar was there too, with a bunch of flowers.

I felt so elated about travelling so far on my own; my confidence went through the ceiling.

Sydney was a wonderful city. Shelley made me feel welcome. It was such a joy to see them all, and my beautiful granddaughter was a delight. This was the medicine I needed.

Paul's mother, who lived in the Sunshine Coast in Queensland, invited us to stay at their home for two weeks.

I will always remember the time Pauline, Paul's mother, met us at the airport. She wore a hat and was extremely smart; she was a very attractive lady with large blue eyes. She was Oscar's ex-wife, and he loved her very much. But she had gone off with their friend about twenty years ago. He never forgave her.

When we arrived at their home, I was in a state of awe when I saw her house. It was built on a hill with a panoramic view. The sea was in the distance.

It was more like a hotel, given the size of it and the way it was built.

As you came up the steps to the double door entrance, the decking went all around the house, passing all the rooms. Some rooms had a patio door leading out onto the decking. Everything was painted white.

The palm trees that surrounded the entrance were magnificent. The plants were tropical. There were birds of paradise, ginger plants and many different types of palms.

There was a swimming pool outside, with a barbecue under an awning that protected you from the strong, glorious, Australian sun.

The room Pauline gave to me was so fresh and clean. I couldn't get over how everything was so white. It was like one would see on a TV ad, advertising paint: the paler side of white, so to speak.

The net curtains were blowing in the wind because the patio door was open a little to let in the breeze that came from the open space outside. When you looked outside you could see above all the trees right out to the sea.

Adjoining the bedroom was a bathroom, which had a toilet,

bidet, washbasin and a shower. The towels were new. Everything was perfect. I was afraid to use the towels because they were so perfectly placed.

Pauline introduced her husband, Robert. He had a beard that was a little on the grey side, a true Ozzie-looking man. He spoke with an Australian accent.

'Pleased to meet you,' he said, holding out his hand.

I thought of saying, 'G'day, mate!' but thought better of it. Instead I said, 'Hello, Robert, pleased to meet you too.' I was thinking, You lucky Ozzie. What a place you have here!

Shelley was in the apartment below. She had a bathroom, a small kitchen, and a lounge leading out to the poolside. It was all so perfect.

Baby Isabelle was two months old, and she was the centre of attention with the doting grandmothers.

I was in another world, away from the hardships of London. I felt I was in paradise.

Pauline and Robert were born-again Christians, and most of the conversation was about their faith.

I love Jesus, but found it hard to believe that the only way to heaven was though Christ. What works for me are the principles of the twelve-step recovery programme and the simple way of believing 'the God of your understanding'. All I had to do was believe in a higher power. That could be anything.

One alcoholic declared that the bus that drove him past the pub was his higher power. It's so simple.

Two weeks passed in no time. Pauline and Robert treated me with the greatest respect, but underneath all the politeness, Pauline was working on Shelley to move to Noosa, where they lived.

We spent a lot of our time looking at houses for sale, in the most beautiful spots. The real estate people knew what they were doing, which was clear when you saw the set-up they had on display.

The plot of land that was for sale was located by a riverside. The few houses that were built were show houses. Pauline stopped by one of the show houses to have a look inside.

It was unbelievable. The design of those houses was the cat's whiskers. Mostly they were open-plan, designed to bring the river to be part of the living room and the bedroom.

The house we looked at was built right next to the water. The walls were of thickened glass. When you were in bed you could look out and see the river. The river was as blue as the sky.

The swimming pool had a built-in jacuzzi next to a jetty leading to a boat.

When I saw the display of the most beautiful homes in the world, as I thought, I was once again in awe of it all. No wonder Shelley wanted to live in Australia! This place, called 'Noosa Waters', was magnificent. Of course, Shelley was taken with the idea of one day having a home like that.

My feelings were all over the place. I couldn't get out of the car when they viewed the second house on the water. It was all too much for me to bear.

I had to go back to England the following week – to what? Emptiness – that's how I felt. I wanted to live in Australia with Shelley and Paul and my granddaughter Isabelle. I kept thinking about Oscar's offer.

Paul had a good thing going for him in Sydney with his boatbuilding business. But Pauline was wise enough to win Shelley's heart to move to the Sunshine Coast with them as their neighbours; she said they would have a better life near them.

Oscar never gave up on me moving to Australia. He took me out to dinner and said he was willing to give up drinking if I would give it a go.

On the journey home, I couldn't help wondering, maybe I should give it a try; and after all, if it didn't work out I could always come back. Australia was a wonderful place to live.

When I got home, I felt lonelier than ever.

I still had my job with the handicapped baby, and I was fostering the young boy, Jerry, and going to two meetings a week at Al-Anon. But I was grieving for my mother and was in need of someone to love me. I hadn't found myself yet, so the old mental disease kicked in.

Go to Australia and leave the past in England…

Oscar kept calling me saying he loved me. He rang me nearly every day. I was feeling vulnerable after my mother died and I missed my family life. The temptation was too great for me to resist.

I gave notice to the social services to end my fostering contract, and gave up my caring job with the baby. I rented my house and said goodbye to my children.

Daisy was pregnant; she didn't give me the impression that she needed me. I hardly got to see them anyway; they lived too far up north. I felt that I wouldn't be missed.

Rosy, on the other hand, didn't have her mother any more, and her children were growing up. She looked to me to fill the empty space Mum's absence left in her life, and she was actually sorry to see me go. She was beginning to show signs of liking me!

The thought of running away and starting a new life in Australia was very strong in my mind now. Nothing was going to stop me.

Once again I travelled across the other side of the world, not knowing what the future held for me.

I rented my house for six months and thought that was enough time to find out if I was doing the right thing or not.

Oscar and Paul met me at Sydney Airport. Oscar was very pleased with himself, thinking he'd got himself a wife.

'Hello, sweetheart!' he said. 'I can't believe you're actually here. How was your journey?'

'Long,' I replied. I was in a kind of daydream, not really knowing what my feelings were. 'How are you, Oscar?' I said.

'I'm very happy to see you.' He bent over and kissed me.

Paul drove us to his father's house and said, 'See you tomorrow, Kate. I'll collect you around noon for Sunday lunch.'

It was Saturday night and I was very tired from my long journey. Oscar showed me to my room and was hopping around like a busy bee, not quite sure what to do to make me feel comfortable.

The house was much smaller than I imagined. It had two bedrooms, a kitchen, living room, a bathroom and a room for Oscar's office.

He was in pharmaceuticals and travelled around supplying drugs to doctors and hospitals. He said, 'I'm so glad you're here, Kate. My house isn't much compared to Pauline's. She took everything when she left me.'

He was very bitter where Pauline was concerned and didn't let anyone forget it.

He made me some tea and showed me around the house and garden.

'It's lovely,' I said. 'I need to get some sleep now, if you don't mind, as I didn't get much on the plane.'

I gave him a kiss on the cheek and went to bed. 'Good night, see you in the morning.'

The next morning I woke early because of the jet lag.

All of a sudden I heard a tapping outside. There was a large bird tapping on the window. It was a crow pecking on the netting. It gave me a start. Then a feeling came over me that I wasn't prepared for. It was a lost feeling, as if I was in limbo land. I had a knot in my stomach and felt, I don't belong here. In a way, it reminded me of the omen I had just before I left Andy.

'Good morning, Kate,' said Oscar. 'Did you sleep well, sweetheart?'

I thought he was a little old-fashioned and very overweight. He was only two years older than myself, but I was used to a younger man.

'Quite well, thank you. I was a bit startled with the big bird pecking away at the window.'

'Oh, dear,' he said, worried that I might be upset.

'Don't worry; I thought it was nice to be woken by the birds. I just hope there aren't any spiders about! I heard there are some nasty ones here.'

'No, you won't see any spiders,' he said, trying to put my mind at ease.

After breakfast Paul came and took us to Shelley's for Sunday lunch. I was happy and relaxed when I was with my family.

Oscar had to go to Queensland for a conference meeting with his company for two weeks, and I stayed with Shelley and Paul. I was glad to spend time with Isabelle, who was nine months old now.

Shelley made me a portfolio. She collected all the information on my experience with the handicapped baby and the teenage fostering. When she'd finished she said, 'This is a good portfolio, Mum; you could get a job in childminding.'

I was amazed at the way Shelley put it all together. I was actually a little proud of myself. 'I wonder if I could find work here in Sydney, Shelley,' I said.

'I have a friend who has a baby the same age as Isabelle. She has to work, and her baby is unhappy in the nursery. I thought of offering to have her, but it would be too much for me to look after two babies. I want to give my full attention to Isabelle. I'll introduce you to her, Mum. There's a mother and baby meeting next Friday; why don't you come?'

I was over the moon to be invited out with my daughter and her friends.

The lady in question was very interested in me. When she heard about how I was trained to gravity-feed the handicapped baby I nursed, she was well impressed.

'Would you be willing to look after Elizabeth for a few hours a week?' she asked.

'Yes, I would love to.'

The next day Shelley's friend brought her husband and baby, Elizabeth, to Shelley's house for an interview. They asked me a few questions and within a short time decided to employ me twice a week, four hours a day. I would earn $50. I'd only been in Australia a week and I had got a job and made friends.

When Oscar came back I had an open mind about making a relationship work with him. I though if I could keep up my Al-Anon meetings, and if Oscar kept on the wagon things might work out.

'I must go to my meetings, Oscar,' I said. 'They're very important to me. I haven't got a car, so do you think you could take me and pick me up?'

Oscar's response to my request wasn't what I expected.

'Why do you have to go to these meeting? You don't live with an alcoholic any more!'

I was a bit annoyed to hear him say that; I was under the impression he understood how important my meeting were to me. Then he said, 'The meeting is about half an hour's drive from here, and then I'll have to wait about to take you home.'

I thought, I must go to my meetings. But I didn't like to ask Oscar if he wasn't happy about taking me. So I didn't go.

A week later, Oscar was becoming a little anxious. He said he missed his wine. When I heard this, I knew that I'd made a mistake getting involved with him. The thought of him drinking gave me a knot in my stomach.

Then I went into a panic attack. I felt that I couldn't breathe.

The weather was very hot. It went up to 100°F at times. Oscar didn't have any air conditioning in his house, and I found myself saying, 'I'm sorry, Oscar; I just can't do this any more. I can't stay. It's not working out – I must go home.'

I suddenly knew that I had made a mistake in coming to Australia. I realised I was running away from the loneliness in England.

I was OK at Shelley's house, but when I was with Oscar I felt lost. I couldn't control my feelings of despair. All I thought about was getting back to England.

I rang Rosy and said, 'I want to come home, Rosy. Can I stay with you until I get my house back?'

Rosy was delighted to hear that I wanted to come back.

'Yes, that will be fine, you can stay with me. I've missed you.'

'Good,' I said. 'I will be home as soon as I can get my tickets changed.'

'Don't leave yet, Mum,' said Shelley when she heard what I was planning to do. 'Stay for a couple of weeks. You're stressed and you need some time to get your head sorted.'

Shelley was a wise soul and was disappointed that her mother was leaving. She was just getting her head around the idea of me being involved with her father-in-law and living nearby.

But I knew she was planning to move to Queensland in the near future, and the thought of being with Oscar without my family around was unthinkable.

Being with Shelley and Isabelle was what kept me there, and the thought of being alone with Oscar was something I knew wasn't meant for me. All my visions of a new life in Australia went out of the window.

As much as I wanted to reciprocate the love Oscar had for me, it just wasn't in the plan of my destiny.

He was so upset; he didn't know what hit him when I said I was going home. The poor fellow got drunk and became depressed. I felt so sorry for him and really bad for hurting him. He said, 'You didn't try hard enough!'

Maybe he was right; but if Shelley had said, 'Stay with me, Mum, until you get settled,' I would have given Australia a chance. Then I might have made a relationship with Oscar, a step at a time. He was a lovely man. But it wasn't meant to be. Shelley had her plans for living in Queensland and having a relationship with her mother-in-law, Pauline. I would have just been in the way.

Two weeks later, Oscar pulled himself together and said his farewells to me at the airport. He said to me, with a loving and sincere heart, 'If you change your mind, Kate, I will always be here for you; I really want what's best for you. I do understand that you miss your family. I will write, and remember, I do love you.'

I was so touched by his kindness. I thought to myself, Well, at least there is someone in this world who loves me! I gave Oscar a kiss goodbye, and felt so relieved that we left as friends.

~28~

On the journey home, I thought about how Oscar had really tried to make me happy, and what a comforting thought it was that I had someone out there who loved me.

Running away from the hardships of my life wasn't what my higher power had in mind for me, but I guess I needed to go to Australia to see that it wasn't meant for me.

I'd had this dream in my head for a new life on the other side of the world and nothing could shift it. This idea was in the way of my spiritual growth.

While I was in the air I got to thinking about my children.

I knew my children loved me, but none of them wanted to take any responsibility for me. I came across as too needy and dependent. They didn't understand how ill I had been.

All I needed was time to heal from the injuries of my past. I thought, I have to earn respect from my children. How can they respect me when I took so much abuse from Andy?

Shelley could hardly believe it when I so freely took him back when he left me for Sally. Missy said, 'Mum, don't let him say those things to you. Why do you put up with it? You should leave him.'

Daisy gave up on me. She thought I was a hopeless case.

Matt felt the pain I went though. He was a bit on the sensitive side. He found it all too painful, seeing his mother in tears most of the time. Being a boy, he felt he should do something about it, but he was much too young to stand up to Andy when he was drunk and out of order. Matt took all the pain inside, and held a grudge against his father – and me – for years to come.

This 'mental disease' affected all my children.

Andy may not have been an alcoholic, but that doesn't really matter. His behaviour was like one when he drank.

Most people think that to be an alcoholic one has to look for a drink first thing in the morning. Or it's a person that sleeps on a park bench. This is true, but there are also alcoholics that can carry on their lives and hide their problem. They can be doctors, solicitors, builders, musicians and housewives. They are everywhere, going about their daily lives, waiting for the next drink and hiding the bottle in the most unlikely places.

Most of them are in denial that they have a problem.

It's said in AA that only 2% of alcoholics have got the disease arrested. It's an illness that society doesn't recognise for what it is, and that is, the person who drinks is powerless and needs help in a way that only another sober alcoholic can give.

The story of Dr Bob and Bill W, the founders of Alcoholic Anonymous, explains it all. Their desire to drink miraculously disappeared when they each shared their own life story with another alcoholic.

The realisation of the harm that Andy and I did to my children was a real eye-opener.

I couldn't expect my children to understand how hard it was for me. They were only children. They depended on me to show them how to live and to teach them right from wrong, and how to grow up into confident and independent people.

But how could I do that? I was too damaged by my childhood. I was still learning to grow up and find myself.

As I was deep in thought, I made a promise to myself: I will make amends to my children, but first I must get well, and I will. I'll do everything I can to be a good mother. I know that I can't turn back the hands of time, but I will show them that I can make a difference to the world for the better. I want to earn their respect. But first I must learn to love and respect myself.

~29~

Rosy met me at the airport at six in the morning. She had a big smile on her face.

'Hi, Kate. I'm so glad you're home. I've really missed you.'

I was so glad to be back in England after the heat in Oz. It was a relief to be able to breathe in the air.

It was cold because it was March, but cold was good. I loved the cold and told myself, I will never complain about the cold weather again.

'Hi, Rosy. It's good to see you. How you been?' I said.

'A bit lonely... Linda is getting married next month.'

Linda is her daughter and has been a great support to Rosy since my mother died.

No wonder my sister wanted me back home. Ricky, her son, was engaged, and he was getting ready to leave the nest.

'Well, I'm home now,' I said, feeling pleased with myself: one, for being back, and two, because Rosy was happy to see me.

It felt good, really good. I thought, Rosy needs me. How bad can that be? She's always been superior, the one in control.

I then remembered the twelve-step programme and how I prayed for the anger and resentment I had toward Rosy to go. At that moment I realised that I had lost the anger I had felt towards her. God works in mysterious ways.

My relationship with Rosy changed from hate to love during the years that followed.

All I need to do now is to lose the resentment I have towards Andy. It wasn't easy to forgive and let go of all the pain of losing all I loved, and the heartbreak when he left me for Sally. There were years of abuse – emotional, sexual and mental abuse – that almost led me to suicide. The anger went deep into my soul; I was powerless over it. At the same time I was willing for God to set me free. I knew that having all that anger wasn't healthy for me.

Although I had a long way to go to get my demons to leave, I was on the right track. To quote from the big book, *Alcoholic Anonymous, The King's Highway*: 'There is a plan for my life that only my soul knows about.'

The first thing I want to do is go to a meeting, I thought. I haven't been to one for over a month now.

At the meeting I talked about my adventure in Australia and how happy I was to be back. I thought, I have to get back to doing my step work and look for a sponsor to help me. But still no one measured up to Jessie.

Rosy made me feel at home. I was delighted to be living in a million-pound house. My house was still being rented out; it had another five months to go.

I'd be happy to stay here with Rosy for five months if she continued to treat me like an honoured guest, I thought. The next thing I must do is get a job. I had the portfolio that Shelley organised for me.

So off I went to a nanny agency and proudly showed them my portfolio. The person in the agency said, 'This is good! You'll be able to get employment as a nanny anywhere.'

My confidence perked up. I felt good about myself. To think, I can get a job anywhere now…

The person in the agency went on, 'My books are filled with people looking for someone like you, a mature lady who has experience with children. I have a position here for you if you want; it's just down the road. This man's wife is expecting and she's having trouble with morning sickness. She's in bed all the time and has two children, a four-year-old and the other eighteen months. The man works from home and needs help. Are you interested, Kate?'

'Sure, I'll give it a try,' I said.

The lady was a bit of an actress, milking it with her husband for attention. There wasn't much wrong with her. In fact she was a right bitch. The previous nanny left because she belittled her.

I had my work cut out dealing with this melodramatic nutcase.

The husband was a dear, trying to please his henpecking wife.

I was good at not letting people get to me. My past experiences had taught me that. So the pregnant woman saw me as a bit of a threat.

When she overheard her husband making polite conversation to me about Australia, she soon got herself together. The man was delighted and said to me, 'I don't know how you did it! My wife has got out of bed at last.'

Then he gave me an envelope with £200 in and a thank you card.

I got my house back before the six-month contract was up because the tenants went back to Italy. I told my sister, 'I'll be able to go home now, Rosy. My house is vacant and I need to do some work on it.'

Rosy encouraged me to stay with her. 'Why don't you stay here with me? It's good to have you around.'

So I went back and forth to my home and started working in the garden again.

The phone rang. It was my son-in-law, John. He sounded a little distressed.

'What's up, John?' I said.

'It's Baby Emily, she's in hospital.'

Daisy's baby was born when I was still in Australia.

'Why, what's happened?'

'Suspected meningitis.' Baby Emily was only six weeks old.

'I'll be up straight away,' I said, sensing a state of emergency.

'OK, come to the house and I'll get the nanny to bring you to the hospital after she picks up Alison from nursery.'

I quickly packed my overnight stuff and drove to Sheffield, praying on the way, Please, God, don't take Emily. Please, Emily, don't leave us, sweetheart. I'll take care of you, please fight, don't give in.' Tears were welling up in my eyes.

I had no idea why I said, 'I'll take care of you.' I must have had some kind of premonition or insight into the future.

It took me three hours to get to Sheffield.

The nanny was with Alison at the house waiting for me. I gave my granddaughter a big hug, and then we headed for the hospital.

Emily was in the intensive care ward, with Daisy and John waiting for the tests to come back. The baby was crying her little heart out. Daisy looked so worried.

Eventually the test proved to be negative. Everyone sighed with relief. Emily had a virus and her temperature was high, but she wasn't in any danger.

I prayed and said, 'Thank you, God, oh, thank you!'

After that scare, Daisy was worried about leaving her baby with anyone. She had to work because there wasn't anyone to whom she could delegate the work she did for the company.

Daisy needed someone to take full-time care of Baby Emily, pick up Alison from the nursery, prepare her lunch, and take care of them until Daisy came home from work. She needed a full-time nanny.

The last nanny had been a young girl who was more interested in painting her nails and speaking on the phone to her boyfriend. She didn't notice how sick Emily was until Daisy came home and found her burning up in her crib.

Daisy was too afraid to leave her baby with a stranger now; she just couldn't take the chance. So I suggested that maybe I could care for Emily. That idea went down well.

It meant that I had to travel up on Tuesdays and then go back home the following Friday. Daisy had them on Saturday, Sunday and Monday. It worked well.

Rosy wasn't too happy, I was away midweek; she thought the deal was, I was a companion in exchange for me staying with her.

That didn't bother me; I was used to Rosy putting her needs before those of others. I wasn't too worried what Rosy thought; I was only too happy to get some bonding with my grandchildren and my daughter, Daisy.

Alison was two now and Emily was six weeks old. They needed caring for and I was delighted to do the caring.

It was quite a task, travelling back and forth on the motorway and looking after two small children, but it was the best thing that could have happened to me for a very long time.

John was grateful for the support. He put me on the books and gave me a wage. Having their minds at ease around their babies was a big relief for him and Daisy.

Sometimes I was taken out to dinner with my daughter and son-in-law. It was a good feeling being apart of a family again.

I thought I'll try out the Al-Anon meeting in Sheffield, but it was a bit daunting travelling across the Peak District on a dark winter's night. The scenery on the way there was beautiful, but at night it was very scary.

I was worried that some alien might abduct me. Strange as it may seem, I believed in mysterious phenomena after watching a documentary on how people had being taken up in a light and were subject to being screened during some mystical occurrence. So I stopped going into Sheffield in the evenings and waited for the weekend to go my meetings.

~30~

Missy was planning to get married, and her father was paying for the wedding. Daisy and John were invited.

Andy hadn't spoken to Daisy since she met John.

He wasn't very happy with Daisy because he said that she had got involved with one of his business clients, and that was against his principles. At least, that was his excuse. The fact was he just didn't want to lose her. She was a great asset to his business.

Missy's wedding broke the ice with Andy and Daisy. They began to talk to each other again. Little did I know how their new bonding would affect me at a later date…

I was a little worried that I would be uncomfortable with Andy at Missy's wedding. I thought, I really need to lose this deep resentment I have towards Andy if I want Missy's wedding to go well.

Missy planned a big wedding. She had four bridesmaids and booked a hotel in Hertfordshire for the reception.

'Mum,' she said; 'I really want you and Dad to get on at my wedding. Do you think you could be friends for just one day? I want to have my wedding day with both my parents sitting at the top table with Gary and myself. I have asked Dad to come without his girlfriend. He said he would be happy to do that. I want to have a day that's about me and Gary, Mum.'

I wanted my daughter to have a happy day too, so I thought, I'd give it my best shot. But I was worried that I might be affected by Andy's presence. I couldn't help thinking that Andy wanted to have his revenge on me. I knew him better than he realised. He was the kind of guy who never let anyone get the better of him. He was very cunning.

He'd wait for as long as it took to get his revenge on me. He was very hurt when I left him. He didn't want to look at his part in it; he just told everyone that I left him for another man.

I thought, I don't trust him and I don't trust myself. The only way I can protect myself from him is to ask my higher power to help me. I needed to be free from any negativity I feel towards him.

The way forward was to get the resentments and anger arrested. This 'mental disease' seems to know how to pierce my heart. It seems to get power from negativity. Resentment and anger form the key that opens the door to the demons that destroy all relationships.

I have struggled with letting the past go for years now. This time, I thought, I must get a sponsor to help me with this problem.

Finding a sponsor wasn't that easy, because it had to be someone who had worked the programme and was living the principles of the twelve steps. What I needed was a spiritual guide.

'Have you ever been to an AA meeting?' Mary said. She was one of the ladies who were at the Al-Anon meeting.

'No, I haven't. Have you?'

'Yes, it's very powerful listening to the alcoholics. They work the programme to stay sober. It's a disease that can kill if they don't get it arrested.'

'Do you know where there is a meeting, then?' I said, with hope in my heart that I may get help there.

'Yes, there is a meeting every Saturday morning in Archway. I'll take you if you like. I'm a member myself; I go to both meetings because my son is a user, and coming here helps me.'

I thought, Great, maybe I'll find a sponsor there.

Saturday morning came, and off I went with Mary to my first open AA meeting.

'Open meeting' meant that anyone was welcome to join in the meeting just as long as they didn't 'share'. It was only the members who were allowed to speak.

I will always remember that first meeting. A kind-faced man greeted me. He was in his late forties.

'Welcome, I'm Bobby,' he said, holding out his hand in a friendly way.

'Hello, I'm Kate,' I said, shaking his hand. 'I don't know if I belong here, my ex-husband is the drinker.'

Then Bobby said with conviction, 'You're in the right place.'

I looked around and noticed that there were as many women in the meeting as there were men; quite a few of them had their children with them.

There was another room adjoining the main room for the children to play while the mothers attended the meeting. The members followed a rota system to look after the children.

The meeting was full; many members were smiling and seemed to be happy with themselves. It was a good feeling to be with happy people. There was a kind of safe feeling in the room, which put me at ease.

The meeting started very much the same way as my Al-Anon meeting.

They read some words from their big book. Then the steps and traditions were read out.

One of the men talked about his experience and explained how he was affected by his addictive drinking and what strength he got from coming to the meetings. He spoke for about twenty minuets. Then the meeting was open for others to come in and share their experiences that related to how it was and how it is for them today.

The idea was to share their experience, strengths and hopes.

This was a step meeting, so they concentrated on the steps. This met with my approval, as I wanted to learn more about the twelve-step recovery programme.

Almost everything that was said in that meeting I related to. I thought, I'm like these people; the only difference is, I don't drink. The way these people feel about themselves is familiar, and how they lost everything because of the drink.

I then began to understand a little more about myself.

I had come from a long line of alcoholics. My grandparents on both sides of my family were alcoholics. I thought, I'm affected by this mental disease. It comes from my parents. This so-called mental disease was in their behaviour patterns that had been passed down from generation to generation. You could say it was contagious.

I was now able to see how this disease had been active in my childhood. I began to understand why I felt so unloved and lonely as a child. It's a cunning disease with a kind of intelligence that gets into your mind. It feeds on the dark side of life.

The drink could have been the way out from my fear of being abandoned, as it was for so many others, but instead I attracted the disease through my relationships. Yes, this meeting was a real eye-opener for me.

Bobby came over to me when the meeting came to an end, and with his big warm smile, he said, 'Did you enjoy the meeting?' Then he suggested I should go with him and a few others to the coffee shop.

'Yes, I did enjoy the meeting,' I said, 'and yes, please, I would love to go and have a coffee with you.'

Then I asked him, 'Have you been coming to these meeting for long?'

'I've been going for over twenty years,' he replied. 'I sponsor a lot a members. It's the way I stay sober. They say you have to give it away to keep it.'

He meant keep the programme working in his life. He went on, 'If it wasn't for these meetings I wouldn't be here to day. This disease is a killer, you know.'

Bobby was a much loved man in the fellowship; he cared for so many newcomers.

I thought, I need a sponsor, but I don't think I should ask him because he's a guy and that's not a good idea; it's not recommended.

Maybe, I thought, he could be my spiritual guide.

I told Bobby how I was having trouble with my anger towards Andy, and how I had tried to let go of the past. He said, 'Do you want him back?'

'No,' I replied.

'Then, let the past go and wish him well.'

That's all Bobby said.

Little did I know that I had just worked the fifth step with Bobby by sharing with him my problem!

The fifth step says, 'Admit to God, to ourselves and to another human being the exact nature of our wrongs; then God will remove all your defects of character, that's if you have the right thinking.'

I had a sincere heart and wanted Missy's wedding to be a

happy day. That must have been the right thinking, because of what happened at the wedding.

I felt a little better after speaking to Bobby; I was hopeful that I would be able to keep my dignity at Missy's wedding, by not letting Andy get to me.

The acid test was yet to come.

Missy's wedding was the following week and I was desperate not to mess it up for her. I was worried what Andy might do, or say, something to upset me.

The wedding day arrived at last, after weeks of preparation. It was a warm sunny day in July.

Missy was so excited. Her white silk dress had embroidery on the cup sleeves and across the top of her neckline down to just below the high waist. The dress was cut to complement her small waistline with a full skirt and a long train.

Her headdress had a diamond tiara and a three-quarter-length netting fabric with specks of sparkling dust scattered all over it. She looked like a princess from a fairy story.

Missy had my wide smile, which displayed the most even white teeth. Her big blue eyes were like her father's. Her most outstanding features are her long, dark, sweeping eyelashes.

The bridesmaids' dresses were a shot silk fabric, mixed with the colours of burgundy and gold.

They were long and lightly decorated, with satin sashes intertwined with small rose buds, some on the waistline and some along the arms of long gloves that went up to the top of their arms, giving an off-the-shoulder effect. They were so well designed they looked as if they had just come out of a fashion magazine.

Andy made sure his daughter had everything she wanted on that day to make a traditional wedding.

The church bells were ringing when Missy arrived with her father in a white vintage Rolls-Royce.

Gary came in a stretch limousine with his best man.

The displays of flowers were tropical, with goldfish swimming around the huge vases on the tables.

The bridesmaids' bouquets were purple orchids. Missy's

bouquet had beautiful coloured orchids and tropical leaves that hung down her dress.

I was very well presented in lilac and blue. My hair was pinned up under a blue hat that matched my shoes and bag. I looked good and was feeling good.

Over 200 people came to the wedding, and another 200 in the evening.

What a challenge that day was for me!

The master of ceremonies did his job well, and the speeches weren't too long. Andy did his speech and made everyone laugh.

Both mothers were presented with a bouquet of flowers.

Then it came to the first dance.

After the bride and groom did their dance, Andy asked me for a dance. It was all so perfect, I got through the day without any snags.

Then in the evening the band was playing and everyone was having a good time.

I was feeling OK. Then, one of Andy's lady-friends arrived. I had to witness him entertaining her. I was already feeling a bit on the outside, because all of his family were in one corner of the room with relations who were a big part of my world.

But now that I was divorced I didn't belong. Missy and Matt stuck around with them, which didn't help. Daisy, John and the children went to bed early.

This was when I started to get a bit wobbly. I said to myself, I must wish him well. Then I repeated to myself over and over again: *I wish you well, I wish you to be happy, I wish you to be well.*

Even though I was saying it through gritted teeth, I kept it up, remembering what Bobby said to me, 'Wish him well and let go.'

Then I found myself dancing and the wobbly feeling went. I was enjoying myself. I danced and laughed with my brother, Danny. The anger wasn't there any more. It was working; God took it away, just as the programme said. The anger was gone. I never felt that dreadful feeling of anger towards Andy again. I was set free, from that day on.

The anger had been replaced by God's love, and I felt light and free.

Once again, I was experiencing a spiritual blessing. My higher power got me through that day. But the next day, I experienced an anticlimax.

All the joy seemed to have disappeared. I was missing my mother, my home and family. It was hard being on my own, watching Andy surrounded by his family and friends.

I took Missy's bouquet to my mother's grave, and as I placed it down on her headstone, I broke down. I fell to my knees, and then I felt as if my whole world had fallen apart. The tears came from deep inside my soul; I sobbed and cried my heart out. I was grieving for the loss of my mother and the loss of my family. It all came out there and then.

I was missing Shelley in Australia.

Matt was in a world of his own. Daisy was miles away. Missy was wrapped up in her father's life, with little or no time for me.

I poured my heart out to God and prayed for him to help me through this lonely time in my life. I wasn't aware, then, that I was letting all the past go.

It was all part of God's plan. Now my inner healing was beginning in a deep and meaningful way.

~31~

The next week I went back to the meeting to tell Bobby how well I'd coped at the wedding and said, 'Thanks, Bobby, for your help. I really did well. I did like you said and wished him well and it worked. I somehow lost the anger and resentment I had towards Andy.'

Bobby gave me a hug and said, 'Well done, keep coming back.'

I wanted to ask him to help me with the rest of the steps but was too shy to ask.

Then one of the members sat next to me and spoke about his wife. He seemed to be upset and angry.

'I just want to get a divorce and get on with my life,' he said. 'I have just found out she's been having an affair with our so-called friend. I don't know how long it's been going on – probably for years, now that I think about it. All the excuses and late nights, I should have guessed.'

I thought, Maybe I should give him my phone number. I know what it's like to go though a divorce.

'Hi, I'm Kate.' He looked surprised when I spoke to him.

'Hello, I'm Terry. I haven't seen you here before,' he said, with a look on his face that showed his sadness about his wife.

'I came here a couple of weeks ago. I haven't long been divorced myself; it really takes it out of you. If you want to talk to someone who's been there and got the T-shirt, here's my phone number. Give me a call, and I'll be happy to share with you any advice that you might need.'

I gave him Rosy's number, seeing that I was now living with her.

'Thanks,' he said. I thought no more of it and forgot all about him until Monday morning.

It was eight in the morning and the phone rang. Rosy answered it. 'Kate, there's some man on the phone asking for you.'

'Hello,' I said, taking the phone from Rosy.

'Hi, it's Terry, I was at the meeting on Saturday. You gave me your phone number. I hope you don't mind me calling you so early.'

I was surprised. I said, 'Hello, Terry. No, I'm an early bird. What can I do for you?'

'I wanted to ask you about my divorce. I'm not sure how I stand about my pension. I don't want to see my pension going to the bloke my wife's involved with.'

I wasn't aware that the real reason he called was because he liked the look of me. He found out from Bobby that I was a free agent. He was interested in me.

After about a ten-minute chat, Rosy got agitated.

She was pacing up and down the hallway giving out signals to me to put the phone down. Then she blurted out, 'I can't have this, using my phone. I want you to put the phone down, *now!*'

If Rosy could have, she would have snatched the phone out of my hand and cut me off there and then.

I was used to Rose's controlling nature, so I said to Terry, 'I can't talk any more – my sister needs to use the phone. Would you like to meet up some time?'

'Yes, I would love to. I finish work at three. Where would you like to meet?'

'Where do you live?'

Terry didn't live very far from me, so we made a date to meet outside a pub we both knew at four o'clock that afternoon.

I was really looking forward to meeting Terry after talking with him on the phone; he sounded like a very nice man.

At last four o'clock came, and I turned up in my old Fiesta car looking good. When I saw Terry as I was parking the car, I noticed how handsome he looked in his brown leather jacket.

He was a big man, tall and stocky, probably weighed about sixteen stone. He was another blue-eyed blond, just like Oscar, except he was much younger, and a cockney.

'Hi, Terry,' I said with a welcoming smile.

'Hi! Do you want to go inside and have a drink?'

'Do you mind if we go in a pub?'

'Why not? I don't have to drink alcohol; I can have a fruit juice.'

'OK then, I'd like a drink.'

We went into the pub and Terry bought me a shandy.

There was something about this guy that I liked. He spoke softly and was a very good listener. I said, 'How long have you being sober?'

'Ten years,' he said.

My mind was working overtime. I was looking for someone to help me with my steps, and he might fit the part.

Sober for ten years and single... well, not yet, but on his way to being.

'I'm looking for a sponsor,' I said shyly. 'Would you be interested in helping me?'

Terry smiled and then said, 'I don't think that would be a good idea, as I may have other ideas in mind. I find you attractive.'

It was then that I realised he was interested in me. I took another look at his manly figure when he went to the bar for another drink and saw a very masculine, handsome gentleman. I weighed up whether I should encourage him or not.

The bait that Terry threw out to me was something I couldn't resist. I took it, hook, line and sinker. I liked him and knew that this was the person I needed in my life. Terry was like a rough diamond.

We talked for hours and finally he said to me, 'Do you like the theatre? Would you like to come with me, some time?'

'That will be lovely. When?'

'I can get tickets from work. I will see what's on and give you a call.'

We became lovers in a very short time. I knew what I wanted, and Terry fit the bill. So I seized the day.

Terry felt the same about me, he wanted me and he wasn't shy in taking me in his arms to kiss me.

He was a gentle lover; he took his time and made sure I was sexually satisfied.

There was something in his eyes when we made love that gave me the feeling that I was loved and it wasn't just about sex.

Terry had a humble way about him that gave me the impression that I was out of his league. When I said to him on our first date, 'Terry, I think you should know I'm a few years older than you,' he said, 'Why, do I have a chance with you?'

I took that statement as a compliment. My age didn't matter at all to him; he thought I was lovely.

I had waited a long time for this kind of romance to come my way. They say that only fools rush in, but I couldn't help falling in love with this guy!

Rosy couldn't handle it. She wanted me for a companion, so she asked me to move out as soon as she saw there was something going on between me and Terry.

I was ready to get on with my own life anyway, so the timing was just right. I moved back home.

Terry was just the medicine I needed. When I was in his arms, I thought, At last, I've found some one who I can put my trust in, and believe he loves me.

He was like a big cuddly bear, and when I was snuggled up to him at night I felt a warm feeling inside that I'd never felt before.

Terry was a spiritual man; he believed in a higher power.

Sometimes he felt like my father, holding me and filling me with the love that I was starved of as a child. I felt as if I was receiving inner healing from him.

I confided in him and told him how troubled I was about getting all the much needed work done in my house. I asked him if I should sell my house and buy a flat.

Terry said, 'I can't say what's best for you, Kate, but I heard a story that may help, if you would like to hear it.'

'Sure, love to, Terry.'

'Well, it goes like this. There was this farmer; he heard that there were diamond mines to be found in the land. So he decided to sell his farm and look for the diamond mines.

'He travelled for years looking for these diamond mines and found nothing. Eventually his money ran out. He was in so much despair that he threw himself over a cliff and died.

'Meantime, the farmer who'd bought his farm was out one day watering his cattle, when he noticed something sparkle in the stream. He picked up a black piece of rock. It was a diamond. As it turned out, there were acres of diamonds on the farm.

'The moral of the story is: the acres of diamonds are on your own doorstep.'

I loved that story, and whenever I felt like giving up and selling, which I did many times, I remembered Terry's story.

As I was working for Daisy in Sheffield, we had time out to think whether we were doing the right thing getting involved. It was tricky, as I was twelve years older than Terry and he hadn't had time to get over his wife.

It was too soon to go from one relationship straight into another, but I was so smitten with Terry I wasn't thinking straight.

A weekend-only relationship was good for us. It made us take it slowly.

A few months later, Daisy found a person that she could train up to do her work. She wanted to spend more time at home with her children. As it happened, this was good timing; I was tired of travelling back and forth on the motorway.

John was showing signs of having had enough of mother-in-law hanging around. He was getting 'mother-in-law claustrophobia'.

Daisy wanted to have her children back full-time, and I wanted to be at home with Terry. All the changes made for perfect timing.

Emily was nine months old now and Alison was 2½ but no one realised just how much Alison would be affected by my absence. She'd become very close to me.

The bonding I had with my grandchildren was also very important to me. It wasn't as easy as we thought. Alison missed her grandmother more than we expected.

Emily was too young to notice that her nanny wasn't there any more; being only nine months old, she soon adjusted to a new carer. Daisy employed a local lady to help her out from time to time.

Alison was a different kettle of fish. She needed me in her life.

Daisy was so busy building up a thriving business, and John wasn't the type of man who got involved with childhood needs. He used his money power to get through all his difficulties. He had plenty of money and bought them everything they needed. But when it came to spending time with them, it was limited. He did love them, but the old saying goes, love is, as love does.

Alison was showing signs of being insecure when I was looking after her. She was acting out the problems Daisy and John were having; she became an angry child and sometimes difficult to deal with. The time I spent with Alison helped a little, because I was able to give her the time and devotion that a two-year-old needed. I gave her a sense of security when I took care of her, so I became a major part in her life.

Daisy, being a devoted mother, was also trying to run a business with her husband. She was split in two, with pleasing John and being a full-time mum. They focused mostly on the pressures of their business, so they were both burnt out after work.

By the time I left, I had assessed the dysfunction between John and Daisy as being quite serious.

Life has a way of history repeating itself. I believe Daisy was heading for the same kind of marriage that I'd had with Andy.

John agreed with Daisy that I should still see the children regularly, and decided I should come and stay once a month. Daisy came with the children down to London sometimes.

Then a problem arose, because Alison despaired every time we said goodbye.

Unfortunately, Daisy and John decided to stop the visits altogether. They didn't say anything to me about their decision. Daisy was getting support from a counsellor, and they came to the conclusion that it would be better if Nanny was off the scene altogether.

I will always remember the time I last saw Alison at the doorway of their beautiful house with Daisy. I was getting into my car to go home. Alison's blue eyes were filled with tears because I was leaving. I drove away, unaware that I wasn't going to be invited to Sheffield again.

Daisy decided to stop my visits, and she didn't call me or come to my home again. They cut me out of their life, just like that.

In retrospect, I thought of the last time Daisy was in London. Missy invited her to have dinner with her. Unbeknown to Daisy, Missy invited Andy.

Daisy and Andy used to be close before she met John. It

wasn't surprising that within a short time they rekindled their relationship. Andy rang her almost daily, telling her how much she meant to him and how he brought her up and cared for her.

If there was ever an error of fact, this was it. Andy used my daughters to alienate me. He was clever at twisting the truth. The 'mental disease' knew what to say to tune in to Daisy's emotional needs, and because he was in the same trade, they had a lot to talk about. Even John encouraged him to visit and become part of his family.

'They are all I have, Terry,' I said. I was full of self-pity.

Terry put his arms around me and held me close and said, 'I know how you feel; I've lost my family too. My ex-wife has stopped my son and daughter from seeing me. She has probably brainwashed them. My son doesn't want to know me, and my daughter stands by her mother.'

Terry had a lot of compassion for me because he was going through the same kind of heartbreak.

I tried talking to Daisy. 'Why, Daisy, why, are you stopping me from seeing my grandchildren?'

The more I spoke to Daisy, the deeper the hole I got myself into. Daisy was more keen on being with her stepfather than with me. She also wanted to work on getting her relationship with her daughter Alison right, and to keep in Andy's good books. She couldn't have a relationship with Andy and me at the same time, so she chose Andy over me.

I wrote her letters. Then the hurt turned to anger.

To think that she put her stepfather before her own mother! I could hardly believe it. I can only imagine that Andy was encouraging it; he had seen the bond I had with Daisy and John at Missy's wedding. I couldn't help but think that this was his way to get his revenge on me.

Why else did Daisy shut me out, and open the door to Andy? Then I heard my inner voice again.

'Kate, it hasn't got any thing to do with you. Daisy has an empty space inside her. It's the space that her father left. She has a need to be loved by a father, even if it's a false love. When you're starving you will eat any kind of food. Daisy is starved of the love of a father.'

I learned how clever the mental disease was. It knew about Daisy's injuries and used Andy to tune in to the empty space that Daisy had.

I was truly grateful for this inner wisdom. But it still hurt, especially the time when Shelley came to England for a visit.

It was Daisy's fortieth birthday, and all the family were invited, including Andy. I was left out. I had a real challenge that weekend with my resentments.

I used the principles in the programme. When anyone offends you, pray for them and ask God to give you the spirit of forgiveness.

I turned to Terry and poured my heart out to him. He just held me in his arms.

I couldn't bear to think that my grandchildren were in Andy's company, and Alison – how she must be missing me! I certainly missed her and Emily.

~32~

Once again my heart was broken and I grieved for the loss of my daughter and two grandchildren. I said to Terry, 'How can I mend my broken heart?'

He smiled and said, 'Welcome to the world. Life is tough!'

I turned to my programme to help me get though yet another difficult time in my life.

Terry took me to the meetings every Saturday morning. The speakers must have been hand-picked by the higher power, because the stories I heard were very encouraging for me, helping me to turn my life around.

I studied the steps, not only to get recovery from my past injuries, but also to help others find their recovery, the twelve-step way.

There are so many people whose lives have been torn apart by this mental disease.

Bobby became my spiritual adviser during the following year; he helped me with the fifth step by listening to my experiences and hardships. He also helped me to see my part in the dysfunctional behaviour.

The fifth step is about, 'Admitting to God, to ourselves and to another human being the exact nature of our wrongs.'[10]

I always felt that, because I wasn't the drinker, I was the one who took on all the bad behaviour, so my wrongs were about my reaction to the unacceptable behaviour. I also needed to see *my* part in the harm I did to myself.

I looked at the long list of behaviours I made when I did step four and admitted my part in it.

'If you are humble and honest you can see where you have been selfish, dishonest, self-seeking and frightened through a

---

[10] 'Step Five' from *Alcoholics Anonymous*, Alcoholics Anonymous World Services, Inc, p59

situation that had not been entirely your fault,' Bobby said.

In my ignorance of this disease, I tried to control and was critical and judgmental towards my husband and all those on my list in step four. I understood what I needed to do. With Bobby's help I worked through step five.

'Are you ready to forgive all those who offended you?' Bobby said.

'I think I have already forgiven everyone, Bobby. If I haven't then I am willing to.'

'I hope you put yourself at the top of the list. If we don't learn to forgive ourselves and love ourselves, we can't love and forgive others.'

I thought that wasn't easy, because my low self-esteem stood in the way. I blamed myself for not getting out of the situation earlier. I should have left Andy long before I did.

I was seeing things in a different light now. Instead of blaming everyone for my hardships, I took responsibility for my part in it all. I was growing up, and realised how I had to make decisions for myself and not to expect others to be responsible for me.

'Well then, Kate,' Bobby said, 'I encourage my sponsee, after we've done our step five, to go home and meditate for a little while, and when you feel ready, think about step six: "Become entirely ready to have God remove all these defects of character."[11]

'If you do feel ready to forgive all those that harmed you, the next step can be done straight away. Then you can go on to step seven: "Humbly ask him to remove our shortcomings." I do this on my knees, Kate. This is because it says "humbly ask".[12] It's up to you, Kate; you don't have to. I will give you this prayer anyway.'

Quote from the AA book:

My creator, I am now willing that you should have all of me, good and bad, I pray that you now remove from me every single defect of character which stands in the way of my usefulness to

[11] 'Step Sex' from *Alcoholics Anonymous*, Alcoholics Anonymous World Services, Inc, p59
[12] 'Step Seven' from *Alcoholics Anonymous*, Alcoholics Anonymous World Services, Inc, p59

you and my fellows. Grant me the strength as I go from here to do your bidding. Amen.[13]

I thanked Bobby for all his help and said, 'I'm happy to move on to the next step.'

I went home and sat quietly for a while, thinking of my trials and tribulations.

Step six was a wise step. 'Become ready for God to remove all these defects of character.'

It took years before I was ready to forgive everyone who had hurt me. I needed time to heal before I could sincerely forgive.

Step four brought my defect into the light.

Step five: I shared with God and Bobby the exact nature of my wrongs. Now I was ready for God to remove all my defects of character.

I was determined to make a better future for myself and make amends to all my children.

I knelt down and humbly prayed the prayer Bobby told me.

Terry was a wonderful support to me during this time of digging deep into my past.

Talking about digging, the garden was coming along a treat. I'd done most of the weeding and related that to the work I was doing in my steps – weeding out my defects.

Terry helped with replacing the front door and windows.

I was feeling really good, now that my home was being transformed.

My inner voice spoke to me again and said, 'The new door symbolises the door that was opened when you chose to ask God in your life. (Step three.)

'The new windows brought in more light. This symbolised the light of God. Where there is light the darkness disappears.' (Step four.)

The universe was mirroring the transformation that was taking place inside my soul.

The knowledge of keeping my side of the street clean no matter what others did (step five) highlighted how this disease

---

[13] 'Step Three Prayer' from *Alcoholics Anonymous*, Alcoholics Anonymous World Services, Inc, p76

had been working in my mind.

Now I could understand that 90% of people have a disease, one way or another, that has been inherited from their past, and no one was to blame.

You can tell when you are affected if you identify with Eckhart Tolle. When he wrote in his book, *Practising the Power of Now* as follows:

> You no longer smell the flowers by the wayside, nor are you aware of the beauty and the miracle of life that unfolds all around you. Are you always trying to get somewhere other than where you are? Is most of your doing just a means to an end?
>
> Is fulfilment always just around the corner? Or confined to short-lived pleasures, such as sex, food, drink drugs or thrills and excitement?
>
> Are you always focused on becoming, achieving and arranging, or alternatively chasing some new thrill or pleasure? Do you believe that if you acquire more things you will become more fulfilled, good enough or psychological complete? Are you waiting for a man or a woman to give meaning to your life?
>
> Your mind then loses its vibrancy, its freshness, and its sense of wonder. The old patterns of thought, emotion, behaviour, reaction and desire are acted out in endless repeat performances, a script in your mind that gives you an identity of sorts but distorts or covers up the reality of the now. The mind then creates an obsession with the future as an escape from the unsatisfactory presence.[14]

I became obsessed with the future, wishing to make a better life for myself. I was a lost soul as far back as I could remember.

Now I have found what I was looking for: me! I am at last at peace. I accept myself just as I am, defects and all.

---

[14] From the book *Practising the Power of Now* copyright 1997 by Eckhart Tolle. Reprinted with permission of New World Library, Novato, CA. www.newworldlibrary.com

~33~

Now that I was connected to my higher power I had a profound and simple knowing that the universal source supplies everything. I was beginning to acquire wisdom, for I had paid the price.

There was one thing I felt sad about, which was my lack of education; it stopped me from developing my God-given talents. I missed out on my achievements in life. Then I thought: I have a choice, I can learn. It's not too late. It's never too late.

I had a desire to learn to type and use a computer, so I went to evening classes.

If you have ever seen the movie *Educating Rita*, then you will understand how I felt when I learned to type. I was elated. I developed a taste for learning. My confidence took a quantum leap. I had a feeling of freedom, as if I'd been let out of a cage.

At first, it took all of my courage to walk into the room of students at the college. My spelling problem made me nervous of confrontation. The palms of my hands were sweating and my heart beat faster, but I brazened it out.

There I was among all the others in front of a computer with headphones on, learning to be a touch-typist.

This was only one of the little miracles that I experienced.

The change in my life was phenomenal. The nervousness went when I read the literature at the meetings. If I couldn't read a word, I simply asked the group. No one was there to judge me. Those meetings were like my family. They listened and supported me immensely.

Going to meetings twice a week helped me to believe in myself. This was because I felt validated; I wasn't a hopeless case after all.

I was beginning to understand that when you change your thinking to being positive, the power of the universe acts as an outside mirror to what's on the inside, and things in your favour come to you and your world.

The power of intention was something that I was now experiencing.

When I was in line with God's will and not my own, I learned that my desires were fulfilled. One of my desires was to see Shelley again and take Terry with me. Shortly after I thought about it, I was booked to go the following Christmas.

In the meantime I wanted to do the next step, step eight:

'Make a list of persons we have harmed and become willing to make amends to them all.'[15]

This is the step where I had to face up to my part of the disease and admit the harm I done to others, whether I meant to or not.

Bobby said, 'Kate, you must be on the top of your list of people to make amends to. If you don't make amends to yourself first, you will probably offend again. It says in this step – become willing – and once again I say to you, "To be willing is the key that opens the door." '

I was already making amends to myself by going to college to improve my education, plus going to the meetings and learning that there is a better way to live, in self-loving.

Now that I was getting in harmony with the universe, I didn't feel guilty about the harm I did to others. I believed that if I acted on guilt it would mean that I was to blame for the dysfunctional behaviour that went on. The mental disease would love that.

It's only by achieving awareness of the way this mental disease works that I will be able to take responsibility for my part in it. Then, all-round forgiveness is necessary.

The step eight list could be set in columns, such as, the people we feel ready to make direct amends to, the people we feel willing to make amends to at a later date, and the people we feel we can't make amends to for today.

I looked at the list I made in step four and was able to see how I acted out in response to my injuries.

My children were those who were most harmed. It was amazing how I could now see now how my behaviour did so much harm to them.

---

[15] 'Step Eight' from *Alcoholics Anonymous*, Alcoholics Anonymous World Services, Inc, p59

Negative thinking is also a big offender. The times I wished harm on Andy when I was angry with him, unaware that the negative energy I sent out wasn't only harmful to him but also harmful to me!

Have you ever seen how three fingers are pointing back to yourself when you point one finger out to others? I believe in the cliché, 'What goes around comes around'.

I wasn't aware that to send out harmful thoughts is also participating in psychological warfare. The mental disease feeds on the perpetrator and victim when negative thinking is in the atmosphere.

'Remember, Kate,' Bobby said, 'if you're not part of the solution, you're part of the problem.'

Andy's sister, Jackie, was one of the people I was angry with. She was so much against me when I married Andy. She encouraged Andy to be with Sally. I put her on the list in the column of those to be willing to make direct amends to at a later date.

I had many enemies. Being married to Andy, who was a wealthy man, put me in the firing line of many jealous women; and Andy, being an outrageous flirt, didn't help at all. He encouraged it.

The thing to do now, after I'd finished writing my list of those I believed I had harmed, was to share it with Bobby. He said, 'Why don't you work on one person at a time?'

It was then that I decided to write a letter to all those who had offended me, all those that I had a resentment against. I began with my father. I wrote to his spirit and told him how hurt I was that he had never shown me any affection, and how angry I was for the way he loved Rose over me. I wrote as if I was speaking to him face to face. I went back as far as I could remember. I wrote about all the things that he did and didn't do that harmed me. Then I said sorry for all the unkind thoughts I had towards him, and that I loved him and how sorry I was for all that was lost between us. At the end of my letter I said I forgave him for everything that I wrote down. Then I asked him to forgive me. I read this letter to Bobby. He suggested that I was to take it home and burn it, to symbolise the sickness that was between us was gone for ever, and I was never to mention it again.

When I felt ready I did the same with my mother, then Rosy and Robert. One by one, I wrote a letter to all those on my list whom I had a resentment against. At the same time I said sorry for my part in it. This was a very powerful way to clean up my house, so to speak.

'Well done! You're ready for step nine now,' Bobby said, when I'd completed my task. "Made direct amends to such people wherever possible, except when to do so would injure them or others."[16] Take your time with this step, Kate.' Bobby said. 'You'll find that when you ask your higher power to help you become willing to make amends, you will be in line with his will, and then God will bring to you the people who are ready to receive your good intentions.'

'How can I make amends to my children?' I asked Bobby.

'Let them go and wish them well,' Bobby said. 'Let them know you love them unconditionally and you will always be there if they need you. Children don't *belong* to you, Kate; they just pass through. Once they have reached an age to be independent, they need you to let them go and make their own way. They have their paths to follow and need to make their own mistakes so they can learn their values and find their own higher power. For as long as you protect them, you will be their higher power. They are individuals and need to live their own lives. If you expect them to take care of your needs, forget it; they don't owe you anything.'

I did make it clear to them how sorry I was for all the harm I ever did to them, such as, crying, telling them I was getting a divorce one moment and that I wasn't the next. It was so bad; I did so much harm to them, showing them my despair and looking to them for comfort. They probably will be affected for many years, maybe for the rest of their lives. I was really sorry for all the wrong I did.

I can't change the past so I will wait, with a willing heart, to see where I could do my amending.

I felt that I would like to show them that I'm no longer that weak woman that put up with unacceptable behaviour. I really want them to have a mother who behaved like one. I knew I had

---

[16] 'Step Nine' from *Alcoholics Anonymous*, Alcoholics Anonymous World Services, Inc, p59

to let them go to live their own lives. I took responsibility for my dysfunctional part in their up bringing. I'd used them for years to fulfil my own needs. I used them to be my life. I expected them to make me their life, to be there for me and take care of me. It was all about *me*. I had a lot of growing up to do.

The mental disease has a field day with all the dysfunctional people who hold resentments towards children, and in turn, the children holding resentments towards their parents for not being perfect.

Bobby said, 'To make amends to your children for the harm done to them while they were growing up is out of your hands now, Kate. All you can do is find your own happiness. The best gift you can give them is your happiness.'

Christmas was drawing close. The trip to Australia was on the horizon, and Terry was really looking forward to it. He was in his element with all the changes in his life. His divorce was over and the concern for his pension went away.

What happened next was the last thing I'd thought could happen. Terry said, 'You know, Kate, I never really made amends to my ex-wife. I think I'll go and see how she is. Maybe I can make peace with her… I miss my children and would love them to come and visit me.'

I was quite happy for Terry to work his programme and didn't think twice about it. That evening he came home looking pleased with himself.

'How did it go?' I said.

'She looked good and was happy to see me. I told her that the reason I was there was because I wanted to say sorry for the things I said to her when I left. She asked me how I was getting on and how good I looked. I told her I was going to Australia in two weeks' time. She offered me some tea and then, from out of the blue, she started to show me all her sexy garments she got from one of those Ann Summers parties! I was taken back at what happened next. She came on to me. She said she still loved me.'

I was dumbstruck. The fact of Terry going back to his ex-wife was the last thing I thought could happen.

Terry's ego was well inflated by the sudden change of emotions he was having. He hadn't expected this to happen and didn't know how he felt. He hadn't really grieved for his marriage because he went straight into a relationship with me.

We'd been together for nearly two years now and the last thing I thought was he could go back to his ex-wife.

I kept quiet about it. The trip to Australia was near, there was packing to be done and presents to be bought. Time was running out. The last thing I wanted to worry about was Terry going back to his ex-wife.

I put it out of my mind and looked forward to our holiday.

~34~

'Come on, Kate, the taxi's here.'

'Have you got the passports, the tickets and the money?'

'It's all here, don't worry. Just get your bags and let's go!'

We closed the door behind us and hoped we hadn't forgotten anything.

'Where yer going to?' the taxi driver said.

We both said excitedly, 'Australia!'

He drove us to the underground station. We went to the airport by train.

Terry was a proper gentleman and wouldn't let me carry the luggage, unless it was really necessary.

Both of us were inexperienced travellers, and even though I'd had been to Australia twice before I was as nervous as hell. Struggling with the luggage, we eventually arrived at the check-in desk well in time for our flight.

Terry was like a little boy when he sat in his seat by the window. He wore an old cap that he called his 'lucky cap' and didn't want to take it off. I said, 'Terry, are you going to wear that hat all the way?' He was very excited about getting on an international airliner.

It was a long, long flight. Thank God for the movies we watched on the small screen in front of us!

After thirteen hours we touched down in Singapore. What a relief it was to get off and stretch our legs.

We decided to do a two-day stop over in Singapore. I thought, We might not have the opportunity again.

The Singapore experience was marvellous. It being Christmas time, the main street was decorated with silver streamers that travelled across the whole street.

There were many shops to see and places of interest to visit.

The night safari was fun. Everyone rode in an open train that slowly travelled around the zoo. The commentator spoke about the animals in a loving way. She tried to educate the visitors about the rainforest, and how the animals were affected by the destruction of the trees for commercial use. Then they showed us the glorious magnificent tigers that are now extinct in the wild. It was a thrilling experience.

At the end of the trip around the zoo, they put on a show with some of the animals. The show involved the audience. Terry was the one they chose to have fun with. He was asked to hold a giant snake, a python. He was in his element when they chose him.

Singapore was a wonderful experience to remember.

I was looking forward to seeing my daughter and grand-daughter, Isabelle, again. She was 2½ now.

Shelley and Paul were still living in their rented house in Noosa. Yes, they did move to the Sunshine Coast near Pauline and Robert. They bought land and were looking into building a house in the near future.

Paul worked as a boatbuilder; Shelley worked part-time in a private school for very young children.

Isabelle went to a nursery for a few hours a couple of times a week.

When Terry was introduced to Shelley, it was a joy to see how he was welcomed.

Terry, being a large man and a bit on the self-conscious side, was overjoyed with the warm reception he received. Paul was very kind and polite as well to him. They became friends straight away.

Noosa is a wonderful place to live. The beach, where holidaymakers from all over Australia come, is simply the best.

There is only one road – Hastings Street – that's famous for the designer shops and restaurants, and walking down it was an experience never to forget.

Most of the restaurants backed onto the beach. Once inside, you had the view of the sea and the entrance to the beach. You could have lunch and watch the surfers riding the waves. If you were lucky you could see a dolphin popping up now and then.

Shelley arranged a party for family and friends. Pauline and Robert came along, and quite a lot of Shelley's friends. I mingled nicely; I was at home with my family and their friends. I loved every minute of it.

Then Shelley said to me, 'Mum, you will never guess who lives ten minutes from here.'

I said, with a look of anticipation on my face, 'Who?'

'Jackie! Andy's sister...'

'No, you're joking, she doesn't!'

'She has invited us to dinner, but she said she doesn't think you will accept the invitation.'

I smiled and thought of my programme and the ninth step. This was my opportunity to make direct amends to her. The higher power had brought her to me, just as Bobby said he would.

'I would love to go, Shelley,' I said.

'Great, I'll give her a call and make the arrangement.'

I told Terry about the miracle of how Jackie lived only ten minutes away.

'How did that happen, Kate?' Terry said.

'I knew she was in Australia. She went with this man who was married to her cousin. Her cousin died of cancer a few years back, and he came to England for a visit and Jackie fell for him and ended up here. Here's my opportunity to make amends to her for all the bad mouthing I did about her.'

'Well, well!' said Terry.

A few days later we all set off to Jackie's house. I was thinking, How can I make amends? What do I say? I started to rehearse what I'd say in my head, but was stuck for words. I didn't want to let her think it was OK, the way she behaved, and I didn't want to judge her. I was basically stuck for words.

It didn't matter, my higher power had it sorted.

When Jackie saw me, she was overjoyed that I had accepted her invite. This was my direct amends – accepting! It was an understatement that I forgave her.

Jackie had been feeling really bad about how she acted towards me, and she was sorry. The relief she had when I came to dinner that night was very powerful. The funny thing was she was so happy that she got paralytically drunk. She was so much like her brother Andy in this.

A few days passed, and then I couldn't help noticing Terry kept making excuses to phone home. It wasn't until he took the phone outside that I began to worry.

'Why do you need to talk outside, Terry?' I asked. He didn't say much; he just shrugged his shoulders. It looked suspicious to me. It wasn't the only time I was uncomfortable. He kept going missing when we went out. He said he needed to find a toilet. Something was going on, and I didn't like it.

I began to worry now. He's calling her, I know he is…

'What's going on Terry?' I asked.

'I don't know what you mean,' he replied.

'You keep disappearing, and I think you're calling Amy.'

'Don't be silly! I'm not calling anyone. I just need to go to the toilet a lot.'

I didn't want to have an argument in front of my daughter, so I kept quiet and didn't mention it again.

Terry didn't disappear so often after that confrontation. But I was uneasy for the rest of the holiday.

Then something happened that was totally unexpected. I got sick.

It started when we got back from the Gold Coast. I had a sore throat to start with. Then I became really hot; I was burning up that night and I thought I was going to die.

The weather wasn't helping, being so hot. I wasn't used to such a high temperature. It didn't help matters at all.

I caught a virus and didn't want anyone to catch it from me, so I remained isolated and stayed in my room away from the family for the next few days, hoping I could shake it off. But no such luck: I was sick.

'I'm not feeling well, Shelley; I need to see a doctor.'

'That's OK, Mum, I'll take you to the surgery.'

'I'm sorry for being a burden. All I need is an antibiotic and I'll soon be back on my feet again.'

'Don't worry, Mum, you can't help being sick. You probably caught a cold.'

Shelley phoned the doctor's surgery and made an appointment for that afternoon.

The doctor tested my chest and gave me some antibiotics and said, 'Give it a few days and you should be OK.'

Terry and I planned to go on a four-day cruise around the Whitsunday Islands the following week, then three days on

Hamilton Island. This was our dream holiday. We also planned to stay overnight in Sydney. We wanted the see Sydney Harbour Bridge and the Opera House on our last day before going home.

I felt a little better after a few days. I had a cough, but felt well enough to go on the cruise.

When we arrived at the airport I couldn't believe my eyes. There was a white stretch limousine waiting to pick us up! It drove us to the cruise boat.

The wonderful trip around the Whitsunday Islands was one of my dreams. It was all I thought it would be. The cruise boat wasn't very big; there were only a few people aboard. It was so romantic.

The people were very friendly, and even the crew had fun with the holidaymakers.

'Terry, this is heavenly, isn't it, darling?' I said. I put the thought of Terry's ex-wife, Amy, at the back of my mind; I didn't want to spoil such a lovely set-up.

The stars at night when we were out at sea were mystical. I said, 'Look, Terry – the Milky Way!'

Terry was in awe of it all. The thing he enjoyed most was the snorkelling in the Barrier Reef.

'You should have seen this fish!' he said to me as he came up from the sea. 'It was this big!' He held his arms out wide.

My cough wasn't getting any better, but it didn't stop me from enjoying the best trip I'd ever been on.

The three days on Hamilton Island was very romantic.

We were upgraded into one of their executive suites overlooking the bay where all the sea sports were taking place. There was waterskiing, surfing, windsurfing and motor jets. Terry said while we were on the balcony on the twelfth floor, 'It's paradise here.'

He held me in his arms and kissed me. We made love in the super-king-size bed and slept. I coughed all though the night.

The next morning we took a look around the island and went to the local restaurant for a bite to eat. I wasn't feeling hungry; I was losing my appetite a bit.

'Come on, Kate, eat up – you haven't had much to eat,' Terry said.

'I'm not very hungry, Terry. Don't worry about me, I'm all right. I just need to drink plenty of water; this heat makes you dehydrate.'

I wasn't all right at all, I was going downhill, and my coughing wasn't getting any better.

When we got back from our trip I said to Shelley, 'I need to see the doctor again. I can't stop coughing and I feel ill.'

We only had two days left, and it was Sunday, so the surgery was closed.

'Shelley, have you got a thermometer? I want to see what my temperature is,' I said.

It was, as I thought, high – very high. Shelley phoned the hospital and they told her to bring me to the emergency department.

Terry was concerned, but little did I know what was going in his mind. He wasn't thinking of my welfare; he was thinking about his ex-wife.

The doctor gave me an injection and told me to go to the surgery in the morning to get an X-ray.

My last day (I thought) in Australia was spent at the doctor's. I had an X-ray and was waiting for the results. Terry and Shelley were waiting with me.

'Come in, Kate, we have the results. Sit down and let's take a look,' the handsome young doctor said, after he'd looked at the X-ray. 'When did you say you were going home?'

'Tomorrow.'

'I'm afraid not. You have advanced pneumonia and need to go into hospital straight away.'

I was very sick. I'd been fighting this disease for three weeks now and was seriously ill. One of my lungs was full and the other was affected, I was actually dying! I wouldn't have made it home if I'd got on that plane.

Terry went home and I stayed in the hospital in intensive care. I was given a vaporiser and was injected every four hours, all through the night. I was fighting for my life.

The strangest thing was I wasn't suffering. I was relieved that I was in good hands; I didn't think that I was that sick. The doctors were amazed at my calmness and serenity.

The room I was in was as good as the private patients' and the medical care I got was sent from heaven. I couldn't have been in a better place. The question was, Why? Why did this happen to me? I couldn't work this one out. What has my higher power got to do with this?

Terry phoned me as soon as he got home, and I couldn't help saying, 'Have you gone back with Amy?'

'No, I haven't.'

I didn't believe him. My intuition was telling me something wasn't right.

Shelley came to visit with Isabelle. They looked as if they had just come out of the sauna, the weather was so hot.

The heatwave started the day after I went into hospital. I was lucky because the hospital had air conditioning.

Shelley was exhausted with the worry of my plight and the hot weather.

One week later, I was discharged and cautioned by the doctor.

'Well, Mrs Richard, your lungs seem to have cleared now, so you can go home. I will give you some medication that you must take daily for seven days. Take things slowly, don't overdo it. It will take about three months for you to get back to normal. Don't forget, easy does it.'

I thanked the doctors and nurses for all their kindness and dedication in getting me back on my feet again.

I was a bit fragile for a while. Every day I got stronger, until I was strong enough to go home.

Three weeks later, I came home. I was so looking forward to seeing Terry. I had a bad feeling about him. He rang me daily, but I still had my doubts about him going back to his ex-wife. I tried to put it out of my mind because Terry said he wasn't seeing her. Why was I not convinced?

There he was, waiting in the arrivals lounge.

'Hi, darling! I'm so happy to see you,' I said.

He gave be a long hug and a kiss and said, 'How are you? I've been so worried! What a to-do, getting pneumonia... what am I to do with you? How are you feeling now?'

'I'm OK, a bit on the weak side. The doctor said it will take three months before I will be my old self again.'

I felt better now I was home and with Terry. I put my fears to the back of my mind.

I kept up my Saturday morning meetings and concentrated on the next step, step nine: 'Make direct amends to such people wherever possible, except if to do so would injure them or others.'

'Step nine is the time for picking up the pieces and looking at the harm done and doing our best to salvage lives that have been affected; there are no buts in this step,' Bobby said.

'You can't say sorry, *but* if you didn't do so-and-so I wouldn't have done so-and-so, you know what I mean, Kate?'

'I understand, Bobby.'

Somehow I instinctively knew what to do when I was in Australia. I was given the opportunity to make direct amends to Jackie. I didn't think about the harm that she had done to me. God gave me the grace to forgive her without judgement. It was a great feeling, letting it all go.

'To be sorry is not enough, Kate; we need to show those who we are making amends to that we have changed. We will become the light that our higher power wants us to be. As I said before Kate, "Let it begin with me." The way forward is making amends to yourself by working this programme.'

I was more eager than ever to work this step, but wasn't sure how to make amends to Rosy and Andy.

Then Bobby said something to me that made sense.

'The best amendment you can do to all those who are on your list is to stop judging them. The greatest catalyst for change in any relationship is complete acceptance; it could be your partner, or whoever you're in a relationship with. Complete acceptance without the need to judge or change them in anyway is all you need to do.'

He went on to say, 'When you can do this, have no judgement and accept everyone just as they are, you will be starving their disease as well as your own.'

I thought, Bobby talks about a disease as an entity that has a right of its own. He said, 'Well, if you think about it Kate, the HIV (Immune Deficiency Virus) that develops into Aids is a disease that we don't know we have until we become very ill. This living entity hides itself in our bodies for years until it works out our immune system. When it's ready, it attacks us and comes in for the kill, so to speak. This killer virus is cunning and has an intelligence of its own. We have being trying to find the cure for years.'

'That's quite a statement, Bobby!'

'Think about it, Kate. This mental disease hides in our ego, preying on our weak spots. We don't know that we have been taken over by it.

'Because our ego isn't rooted in a spiritual foundation, its needs are endless and it feels vulnerable. Problems and stress are what uphold and strengthen it. Therefore, some people don't want to be free of their problems, because they do not know who they really are; they're in denial. To be free of problems would mean a *sense of loss of self* to them.'

'Wow! Bobby, where did you learn all this stuff?'

'I have read Eckhart Tolle's book, *The Power of Now*. You should read it. He talks about all this kind of stuff, and I have been around the rooms long enough to see this mental disease working in my sponsees. It certainly had its way with me in my drinking years.'

'It's an eye-opener for me too, Bobby. How do I know when this mental disease is attacking my mind?'

'When you have lost your peace and become confused and angry, and if you find yourself worrying about the future or thinking about the past in a negative way.

'I agree with Eckhart Tolle. He said:

This disease is like a parasite and feeds from our life energy by using our thinking patterning and if we are in our ego edge God out, we are always looking for something or someone to fulfil us, because we are disconnected from our source.'[17]

'Bobby,' I said, 'are you saying to me that there is a disease that works in our mind and is fed by our behaviour?'

---

[17] From the book *The Power of Now* copyright 1997 by Eckhart Tolle. Reprinted with permission of New World Library, Novato, CA. www.newworldlibrary.com

'It sounds insane, doesn't it, Kate? But have you ever seen those mad people who are talking out loud to themselves? Well, if you think about it, that's what we do inside our minds. Most of us are chatting inside our head. It's as if we are possessed; we can't stop the constant chatter.[18] I have a copy of *The Power of Now*. It tells you all about the mental disease.'

Bobby handed me his book, and I said, 'Thanks, Bobby! Well, this gives me food for thought. Do you think this is why so many people are taking substances to try to block it out?'

'You bet! This disease is cunning and devious and shows no mercy. It destroys relationships and tears families apart. The more you create stress, especially emotional stress, the more you feed it. This is what I believe, and I have experienced its treacherous destruction for most of my life, until I was given the wisdom of being conscious of it as not being me. My higher power and working step one helps me on a daily basis to be aware of this disease as a disease, and my powerlessness over it.'

When I heard all this, my inner spirit seemed to know that Bobby was speaking the truth. It was as if something inside me said, *Yes, this is true.*

---

[18] Paraphrased from the book *The Power of Now* copyright 1997 by Eckhart Tolle. Reprinted with permission of New World Library, Novato, CA. www.newworldlibrary.com

~35~

The idea that I have – to watch myself and not to judge anyone, even Andy – gave me a good feeling inside. This is a way of making amends that I can handle, I thought. I just couldn't see myself going up to Andy and saying, 'Hi, Andy, sorry for all the harm I did to you when we were married.'

I was torn to pieces when he abandoned me for Sally.

Then there was Robert; I was left to bring up our two children without any financial support on my own, and his lover writing that dreadful letter… It's hard enough to forgive, let alone make amends. Something else Bobby said that was helpful was, 'God will bring to you, all those who are ready to receive your good intentions. You will instinctively know what's right or wrong.'

It wasn't me who was working this step, it was my higher power. All I had to do was let him. This is God's plan to set me free from this mental disease.

Bobby went on to say, 'When you accept everyone without judgement, this immediately takes you beyond the ego. All the mind games and addictive clinging are then over. There are no victims and no perpetrator, no accuser and no accused.'

Then I said, 'What about the second part of this step, which suggests, "Except where to do so would injure them or others"?'

Bobby's answer was, 'Think about the people who might go up to someone and say, "Sorry, I slept with your wife or husband."

'You have to be vigilant. It would be best for all concerned to say nothing if you had an affair. Also you must find it in your heart to forgive those who have been unfaithful to you. Making amends by forgiving no matter what happened in the past sets you free.'

The St Francis prayer says, 'It is by forgiving, that one is forgiven. Changed behaviour indicates stronger amends than words can say.'

Well, I was about to be put to the test. Terry at last came out with the truth. He had been seeing his ex-wife for the past three months. I was right, he was calling her when we were on holiday in Australia.

Maybe this was why I was ill; maybe I was being given a sign. I will never know.

Not only was I dangerously ill with pneumonia, but I also had a car accident that could have been fatal.

I was happily driving along the motorway doing about 60 mph when a very large lorry pulled out from my left side. The driver didn't see me in his mirror. It was a foreign lorry. The steering wheel was on the left side. He clipped the back of my car and I did a spin in the middle of the road, travelling across the front of the lorry, and it hit me again. Then I spun around, facing the traffic in the wrong direction. At that moment in time, I thought it was the end of my life, and simply waited to have a collision with an oncoming car.

But to my astonishment, my car went into the barrier and I came to a halt at the side of the road. I knew then, when I stopped, that I had experienced a miracle, because I got out completely unharmed. I prayed, 'Thank you, God, thank you!'

I had to ask myself, Has this anything to do with Terry having an affair with his ex-wife? Was I being given a wake up call, or was Terry's ex-wife putting a curse on me? I'll never know. I wasn't a stranger to women in my life who had a problem with my existence.

I wasn't surprised when Terry said, 'I'm going back to Amy.'

I felt the world drop out from under my feet. I said, 'No, Terry, don't tell me you're leaving me!'

He was sad to have hurt me and said, 'I really do have to thank you for teaching me so much, the places I've been, the things I've done. I couldn't have done them without you; I will always love you. But I want my family back.'

I understood about wanting to rekindle his family life. It's a very powerful emotion.

Family life is very important. Most of us have our visions and expectations of what we want life to be. I knew Terry had to follow his dream. I would have done the same if Andy said to me,

'I'm sorry for all the wrongs that I have done, I will stop drinking,' and then admitted he had a problem and said, 'I'll get help.' All I ever wanted in life was a family where we loved each other.

The following weeks were very sad for me. I missed Terry very much. We had been together for two years. I believed he was the only man in my life who really loved me. Then I realised I'd thought that about all the men in my life who loved me and then left me.

Three months passed and I cried nearly every day. But God was good: when one door closed, one opened.

Matt, my son, asked if he could move in with me until he got himself sorted. He was involved with a self-help fellowship himself; therefore he was a great support, and such an inspiration to me.

'Let it out, Mum,' he'd say. When he saw how heartbroken I was, he said, 'You will feel so much better when you let it go. I've learned it's the only way to get better. You have to grieve for the past. Don't suppress your feelings, they have to be felt.'

Here was my son telling me how to get well! How did that come about? I'm supposed to be getting better to show him I'm together. The last thing I wanted was to show my grief to my son. He'd had enough of that when he was young.

I couldn't help it, the tears just kept coming.

'You know, Mum, this kind of grief doesn't just belong to Terry leaving you. I know, I've been getting help with my stuff. It's childhood regression you're getting in touch with. It's painful, but necessary if you want to get better. Don't worry about me; go for it, you're being blessed. Some people pay counsellors a fortune to get to where you are!'

Well, who would have thought that my son had so much wisdom?

I picked up a book that supported Matt's theory. It was a great support, it said that I must go into my grief and feel the pain. I had my inner voice saying to me, 'I'm with you, I am healing you, let go and let God.'

Something very profound was happening to me. God was touching me. I had a knowing in my heart that what was happening to me was meant to happen.

I also believe that God sent Matt to me to help me through it.

It's a strange world when you think about it. I wanted to be strong for my children, and here was one of my children being strong for me. They say what goes around comes around...

I was holding on to the words that Bobby taught me, 'Wish him well and let him go.' I did this every day. Then one day I said to myself, 'That's enough – I'm not going to cry any more; I'm going to move on.'

I went to my meetings and talked with the group about my experiences, especially about what I had learned about the twelve steps.

Not many people have worked their steps, so I became a big attraction to those who wanted to go down the same road as me.

'Will you be my sponsor?' I was asked. I had one person after the other asking me to sponsor them.

I was happy with my life. Matt was at home and I was getting some money from my pension, as I was now sixty years old. Oh, dear, where have the years gone?

Then one day out of the blue, Terry called and asked how I was doing, and would I like to meet him for a coffee.

'It's good to see you, Terry,' I said to him. 'How's it going with Amy?'

'It's not! Things haven't changed, she's still seeing the other man. I think she wants to have both of us in her life.'

I was sympathetic, but somehow I knew it wouldn't work. People don't change, the same old merry-go-round goes on and on. I've been there and got the T-shirt, so to speak.

'What are you planning to do, Terry?'

'Dunno. I'm in debt for £1,000; I haven't got enough to put down on a room.'

'Why did she want you back and then still have the other man in her life?' I asked.

'He's married and won't leave his wife,' Terry answered.

'It looks like she used you,' I said, feeling rather pleased with myself for being in a situation where I wasn't bothered what went on with Terry and his ex.

Terry said, 'Amy was saying all the time that I was thinking of you.'

I'd heard enough; I knew what Terry wanted. He wanted to come back to me.

I still loved him, and life would be much easier with him in it. He did say he still loved me. I believed him. I do understand how hard it is to let the past go, and I understood that Terry had to give it one more try.

We got back together again. I believe, if you let the butterfly go and if it comes back, it's here to stay.

Terry and I have a much healthier relationship now, because the difference in me is phenomenal. I had reached the state of enlightenment where I lost the self that I needed to protect, defend or feed. I wasn't worried what Terry did with his ex-wife; I wasn't bothered with any outside controversy. My soul was at peace with life now, on life's terms. This was the beginning of my inner freedom. My head was clear and I was in control of my emotions. I do believe I had inner transformation when I was grieving during those past three months.

In retrospect, when I first met Terry, I sometimes related to him as a father figure. Therefore, when he left the child within me felt abandoned again. That's why the grief I had went so deep. It was my inner child grief. I was unconscious of being brought into the light of God's love and grace to enter. It was all part of God's plan.

Step nine was the end of my old way of thinking.

There are twelve promises that belong to step nine that I feel are God's gift to me they come from the Alcoholics Anonymous book:

We are going to know a new freedom, a new happiness.

We will not regret the past, nor wish to shut the door on it.

We will comprehend the word serenity.

We will know peace.

No matter how far down the scale we have gone, we will see how our experiences can benefit others.

That feeling of uselessness and self-pity will disappear.

We will lose interest in selfish things and gain interest in our fellows.

Self-seeking will slip away.

Our whole attitude and outlook upon life will change.

Fear of people and economic insecurity will leave us.

We will intuitively know how to handle situations which used to baffle us.

We will suddenly realise that God is doing for us what we could not do for ourselves.[19]

I was on my way to the life I prayed for, a life without the emotional pain and fear of mere survival.

---

[19] *Alcoholics Anonymous*, Alcoholics Anonymous World Services, Inc, pp83–84

~36~

The winds of change were blowing again; Missy had an announcement to make. She was pregnant!

The relationship I had with Missy changed from that moment on. She rang me almost every day. I guess a baby is the best way to bring a mother and daughter together.

It had been almost ten years that we had an estranged relationship, and I almost gave up hope.

I thought I'd lost her for good. I was joyful, but wary. I didn't want to set myself up for rejection, like I did with Daisy.

It took no time at all to rekindle my relationship with Missy. My new way of thinking helped tremendously. I was able to let the past go and I learned not to judge and to forgive. I was optimistic and had a healthy, loving relationship with her. The main change in me that helped my relationship with Missy was my resolution concerning her father, Andy. I was willing not to say anything about him that related to the past.

My house was looking in good order, after Terry and I finished the decorating, and I believed this was the outside mirroring how my everyday life was in harmony with the universe. The twelve-step programme was working for me.

The next step is what they call the maintenance step.

Step ten: 'Continued to take personal inventory and, when we were wrong, promptly admitted it.'[20]

'This is the step where we have done most of the work towards recovery,' Bobby said. 'This step is about how to maintain your progress. If you like, since you like gardening you can compare this step with a gardener taking care of his much loved garden.

'You know that to keep a garden in good order is hard work.

---

[20] 'Step Ten' from *Alcoholics Anonymous*, Alcoholics Anonymous World Services, Inc, pp59

But the joy that one gets when you reap the benefits is so rewarding.'

'I know, Bobby,' I said. 'I work in my garden for hours to get it looking good. This is where I feel closest to my higher power.'

Then Bobby said, 'Once the garden is in good order, you need to maintain the ground and the plants. There are always weeds that need to be pulled up. The plants need watering and feeding.'

'That's a good analogy of our life situation; I need to watch out for the negative thinking that can pop up from time to time in my mind,' I said.

'Yes, they need to be pulled out before they take root and take over your mind and let the demons in. This is what step ten is about: "Continue to take personal inventory."

'Watch out for the signs, when something goes wrong or there is some kind of loss or upset. Because when the challenges come and they will, we have an automatic, involuntary, conditioned reaction.'

'What do you mean – automatic, involuntary conditioned reaction?' I said.

'Have you experienced your mind playing the same old tune, like, "She did so-and-so, or he didn't do this, that or the other"? You know, Kate, negative thinking. We are human, and the human part of us will complain, judge and gossip. Our minds are like a computer. When you download a program, all you have to do is open it up and automatically the program comes up on the screen, just as it is with our minds. When challenges come and we are in our ego and not in line with God's will for us, we can't help but trigger off our stinking thinking – the same old patterns that go over and over in our minds.'

'What do I do if that happens?'

'Then try to focus as much as you can on your breathing, then say the serenity prayer. Any delay will allow a conditional thought or an old emotion to arise and take you over.'

'Is that the reason step ten says, "When we are wrong we should *promptly* admit it"?'

'Yes, listen to your inner voice, not your mind. The mind can be in your ego, whereas your inner voice comes from the source. There's infinitely more intelligence in your inner being than in your mind. If you can remember, Kate, the most important thing to do when your mind is chatting away is to be still and think, Am I in my ego or in God's will?'

Bobby was a great spiritual guide; he had so much wisdom.

I did want to keep the radical change in me, so I went over my day every night before I went to sleep. Did I do anything to offend anyone? Have I said or done anything that was unkind? Have I judged or criticised anyone?

My tenth step needed to be done daily. Now, I keep my body clean and brush my teeth before I go to bed and when I get up in the morning. Working step ten is how I kept my *mind* clean. The feeling of gratitude I had, morning and night, was effortless. I lost that dreadful feeling of, 'Oh, no, not another day!'

Missy had a girl and they named her Anne. I was included in all the joy of welcoming her in the world. Missy was insistent that I was there when she was born.

I had my daughter back, and the icing on the cake was Anne.

The birth of Anne was one of the best things that happened to me. I was with her almost every day. She became the medicine I needed to fill the empty space that losing my family left.

Anne grew to love me far beyond my wildest dreams.

Missy encouraged me to be as important to her, as she was. My baby granddaughter loved me, and it was unconditional. Missy made it clear to me that she would never hurt me the way I was hurt by Daisy.

I may have been a dysfunctional mother, but I am a grandmother who can be remembered for her wisdom and strength.

Terry and I went back to Australia the following spring.

This time we got a bit adventurous. We hired a car and drove to the Gold Coast in New South Wales. We drove from Queensland, along the old Bruce Highway and the Pacific Highway. I was the driver. Terry had never learned to drive. I can't tell you what a challenge that was. It was like winning a marathon. The sense of achievement and independence in hiring a car and travelling all that way in a foreign country was something that, a few years back, I could never have contemplated happening.

This was one of my miracles.

We had a great time there. We stayed in the Nara Hotel. It was part of the famous 'Sea World' resort. We met my cousin Johnny and his wife, Lisa, in the foyer.

Aunt May, my mother's sister, was Johnny's mother. She and her husband, Jack, and Johnny emigrated to Australia years back.

Many British people went on the £10 deal with little or nothing in their pockets. Aunt May was one of them. Unfortunately, May passed away when she was only sixty years old.

I wished she could have seen how her son became a success in the fashion trade in Australia.

'Hi, Katie!' he called out when he saw me for the first time in many years.

'Hello, Johnny!' We gave each other a big hug, and I said, 'This is Terry, the new man in my life.'

They shook hands and Johnny said, 'Good on yer, mate; it's good to meet yer.' Terry was trying to be friendly by imitating their Australian accent. Johnny smiled, as he was used to that kind of thing.

I was introduced to Lisa. We had a few moments of nostalgia, then Johnny told me all about his life in Australia.

He had two daughters. One was married with three children. The other became a well-known model, and then went on to be a popular TV celebrity.

I was so proud of him. He showed me photos of his beautiful family and I had to think about how my Aunt May, bless her, had thought she was the ugly one. If only she could have seen how beautiful her grandchildren were!

Terry and I stayed for the weekend in Sea World and enjoyed all the fun of the parks e.g. Movie World.

We went to the casino and did a little gambling. Johnny got himself thrown out for being too loud.

I will always remember that night. Terry and Johnny exchanged their shirts and went back in. They would have got away with it if it weren't for Johnny complaining about some machine not working. He brazenly went to the very man who'd thrown him out. The bouncer said, 'I've just thrown you out!' Then he marched him down the stairs once again.

We all ended up in a restaurant in the casino.

There were some twelve-step meetings in the Gold Coast that Terry and I went to.

The strangest thing happened at one of those meetings. A man whom Terry knew well tapped him on the shoulder and said, 'Hi, Terry, fancy seeing you here!'

It was a time to enjoy the amazing things that God was doing in Australia. The meetings there were not much different from ours at home in England. The 'mental disease' was all over the world.

The only downside of going to Australia was leaving.

Isabelle became very upset when we left. I thought, If only they lived back home… My heart was torn between my beautiful grandchildren. I had to let go and accept that Shelley had made her life in Australia with Paul and his family, where they were happy.

When I got back from my six weeks holiday in Australia, Missy was more than happy to see me. Her back was hurting. She had injured it by lifting the baby in and out of the cot.

The business of working and nursing the baby was a tall order; she was finding it hard to cope with all that was expected of her. Running their own business and nursing a small child was a handful. I got back just in time to help. Talk about timing! Missy's back gave out the moment she opened the door to me.

Anne was so excited to see me.

It was good to be home to do my part in helping my family.

This, to me, was God bringing to me the people who were ready to receive my amends.

As I have mentioned before, one of my talents is sewing. Therefore Gary, my son-in-law, asked me if I could help out in their shoe repairing shop doing the stitching.

The shoe repairer was limited in that kind of work, so I stepped in and was happy to be working again.

I fixed handbags and replaced zips in boots. I did all sorts of bits and pieces. I took care of Anne for two days a week while Missy worked in the office, and worked two days a week in their shop.

I was living my dream. I was working my programme and helping others that were travelling down the same road I was.

I was ready to do the next step now, step eleven: 'Sought through prayer and meditation to improve our conscious contact with God, as we understood him, praying only for knowledge of His will for us and the power to carry that out.'[21]

Meditating: it wasn't easy at first, as my mind was always chatting away. The more I tried to quieten my mind the harder it became. I needed to pray first.

The St Francis prayer is a good way to get in line with God consciousness. In fact this was the step eleven prayer that the AA meetings used.

Lord, make me a channel of thy peace, that where there is hatred, I may bring love. That where there is wrong, I may bring the spirit of forgiveness. That where there is discord, I may bring harmony. That where there is error, I may bring truth. That where there is doubt, I may bring faith. That where there is despair, I may bring hope. That where there are shadows, I may bring light. That where there is sadness, I may bring joy.

Lord, grant that I may seek rather to comfort, than be comforted. To understand than to be understood. To love, than to be loved.

For it is by self-forgetting, that one finds. It's by forgiving that one is forgiven. It is by dying that one awakens to eternal life.[22]

Meditating became easier to me after I prayed that wonderful and powerful prayer.

I meditated by giving my attention to my breathing as it moves in and out of my body. I close my eyes and visualise being surrounded by a light; I then mentally breathe in that light and fill my body, making it luminous. Then gradually I focus on my feelings, making sure not to get attached to any visual image. At that moment I experience being in the now, the present moment. All attachments to the past and future are now relinquished. In

---

[21] 'Step Eleven' from *Alcoholics Anonymous*, Alcoholics Anonymous World Services, Inc, pp83–4

[22] 'St Francis Prayer' from *Twelve Steps and Twelve Traditions*, Alcoholics Anonymous World Services, Inc, pp101–2

this state of presence I become free of thought yet still alert.

Here's an interesting experiment from Eckhart Tolle's book, *The Power of Now*:

> Close your eyes and say to yourself, 'I wonder what my next thought will be.' Then become very alert and wait for the next thought. Be like the cat watching a mouse hole. What thought is going to come out of the mouse hole? Try it now. Well? As long as you are in a state of intense presence, you are free of thought.[23]

I soon learned how to talk to God. I've been doing it for years and wasn't aware of it. Now, I have learned how to listen to my higher power, and if I had a specific purpose the easiest way is to stop thinking for a moment. Then I focus on the stillness of my inner energy field, and when I resume thinking I have a clear message that is relevant to my request.

Having a conscious contact with God and my inner body is something like the roots of a tree that go deep into the earth.

When I went to Sunday school, I was told of a parable that Jesus told: there were two men who built a house. One man built on the sand, without foundation, and when the storms and floods came, the house was swept away. The other man dug deep until he reached the rock. Then he built his house, which was not swept away by the floods.

When I was born, I wasn't given a blueprint for building my life. It was as the parable said: I built my life on the sand.

Not any more! Now I have a programme, that's my foundation.

I now go on my merry way, living my life and being connected to my higher power. I was unaware that everyone I came in contact with was touched by my presence and was affected by the peace that I emanated, and this was not based on me doing anything, but just being myself.

---

[23] From the book *The Power of Now* copyright 1997 by Eckhart Tolle. Reprinted with permission of New World Library, Novato, CA. www.newworldlibrary.com

~37~

Step twelve states: 'After having a spiritual awaking as the results of these steps, we try to carry this message to others, and to practise these principles in all our affairs.'

The most precious gift I can give is to listen, truly listen without my mind interfering. Then I'm giving space to the other person; space to be able to hear their own inner voice and inner guide.

Most people don't know how to listen because the major part of their attention is taken up by thinking. They pay more attention to that than to what the other person is saying, and none at all to what really matters.

As far as inner transformation is concerned, there is nothing I can do about it. I cannot transform myself and I certainly cannot transform anyone else. All I can do is create a space for transformation to happen, and for love and grace to enter.

Whenever the challenges of the present bring out the madness in you and your partner, be glad. What was unconscious is being brought up into the light. It's an opportunity for you to bring to the present the unconscious past in you. Only the present can bring out the past. In other words, the future challenges can free us of the past.

I am privileged to have reached this step. It's a blessing from God; I prayed for strength and wisdom when I was a small child. My journey was long and painful.

When I left Andy, I remembered how afraid I was, and the vision that I had of getting on a train feeling like an emotional five-year-old. I didn't know where I was going. The blinds were down and I was alone.

I can't say that I have reached my destination, because I believe that for as long as I'm alive I'm learning more and more about this wonderful world.

The train I visualised years ago symbolised my life journey.

Now the blinds are up, I can see and enjoy the world around me, because I feel connected to it all.

I have a completely new way of living, a state of being permanently connected with the God of my understanding – my higher power.

I have a depth to my life that I have never known before.

I was inspired by the book written by Wayne W Dyer, *The Power of Intention*. I'd like to quote some of the wisdom that I can identify with:

I feel in harmony with the universal field of intention. I don't allow myself to be negative. I have a knowing that the universe source supplies everything. I find that when I say I intend to create something, I will know it will work out. I refuse to think about what can't happen, because I'll attract exactly what I think about. Therefore I only think about what I know will happen. I don't relate to the concept of failure or it's impossible.

I know and trust an invisible force that's all providing and has infinite supply.

My aura seems to protect me from anything that is not from my creator.

I believe in synchronicity, I have experienced that if I want something, such as a book.

Someone turns up who I have been thinking about, or if I need money or information, somehow it mysteriously shows up.

I don't ask for anything because I know that it seems to give power to what's missing.

I have gratitude for all that's present, knowing that this empowers my intention precisely to what I need.

I now appreciate all of nature, rainy days as much as sunny days, the snow and the wind and the sounds of nature.

I feel a connection to all beings and feel hurt by another's pain.

I appreciate the entire world and an affinity to all life as well as to the source of all life.

My peacefulness causes others to feel calm and assured.

I choose to feel good, regardless of what's going on around me.

I know that feeling bad is a choice, and if I feel bad this is an indicator that it's time to change my energy level so that it matches up with the peaceful, loving energy of the source. All I need to do is repeat to myself, I want to feel good.

I choose to reside within myself love, peace, kindness and abundance.

My feeling bad will only ensure that I attract more of feeling bad into my life.

I don't experience the feeling of being separate from anyone. I feel aligned to everything in the universe.

I can see what it is I want to manifest in my life as if it had already materialised.

I say to you that my thoughts when harmonised with the field of intention are God's thoughts, and this is how I choose to think.

If you ask me what can I do to make your desires come true I'll say to you, Change the way you look at things and the things you look at will change.[24]

I would like to end with a parable from another book that inspires me, *The Power of Now* by Eckhart Tolle.

A beggar had been sitting by the side of the road for over thirty years. One day a stranger walked by.

'Spare some change?' mumbled the beggar, mechanically holding out his old baseball cap.

'I have nothing to give you,' said the stranger. Then he asked, 'What's that you are sitting on?'

'Nothing,' replied the beggar. 'Just an old box I have been sitting on for as long as I can remember.'

'Ever looked inside?' asked the stranger.

'No,' said the beggar, 'What's the point – there's nothing in there.'

'Have a look inside,' said the stranger. The beggar managed to pry the lid open. With astonishment, disbelief and elation, he saw that the box was filled with gold.

I am that stranger who has nothing to give you and who is telling you to look inside. Not inside any box, as in the parable, but somewhere even closer: inside yourself.[25]

I can now say that I know who I am, and I thank all those who helped me on my path of recovery; my father and mother, my

[24] Wayne W Dyer, *The Power of Intention*, copyright 2004, Hay House, Inc., Carlsbad, CA

[25] From the book *The Power of Now* copyright 1997 by Eckhart Tolle. Reprinted with permission of New World Library, Novato, CA. www.newworldlibrary.com

sister, my brothers my husbands and children, my in-laws and friends. I am grateful to my sponsors, Jessie and Bobby, and my sponsees for giving me the opportunity to keep the faith; and the people I met in the meetings and all the books that inspired me.

I have experienced a life that I didn't want; now I can choose a life, that I do.

I paid the price of wisdom in order to know the difference. I chose not to be a victim, not to have self-pity, not to struggle to survive. I chose to be happy and love myself and others unconditionally.

That's all, folks.

Bibliography

Alcoholics Anonymous World Services, Inc, *Alcoholics Anonymous*, (third edition new and revised), Great Britain: Hazell Watson and Viney Ltd, BPCC group, Aylesbury, Bucks, 1979

Alcoholics Anonymous World Services, Inc, *Twelve Steps and Twelve Traditions*, Great Britain and Ireland, 1952, 1953

Chronicle Encyclopaedia of History. Part of a 24-disc CD-ROM Library programme from the Daily Mail, catalogue number 0583d

Dyer, Dr Wayne W, *The Power of Intention*, USA: Hay House, Inc., 2004

Hay, Louise L, *You Can Heal Your Life*, USA: Hay House, Inc., 1984

Hill, Maureen, *Britain at War: Unseen Archives*, Bath: Parragon Plus, 2002

Peck, M Scott, *The Road Less Travelled*, London: Arrow Books, 1990

Tolle, Eckhart, *The Power of Now*, USA: New World Library, 2001

Tolle, Eckhart, *Practising The Power of Now*, Great Britain: Hodder & Stoughton, 2002

Lightning Source UK Ltd.
Milton Keynes UK
20 November 2009

146502UK00001B/24/P

9 781847 486103